Minna no NihongoI

みんなの日本語

初級I 翻訳・文法解説 英語版
Translation & Grammatical Notes

スリーエーネットワーク

Published by 3A Corporation
Shoei Bldg., 6-3, Sarugaku-cho 2-chome, Chiyoda-ku, Tokyo 101-0064, Japan

ISBN4-88319-107-9 C0081

First published 1998
Printed in Japan

FOREWORD

As the title **Minna no Nihongo** indicates, this book has been designed to make the study of Japanese as enjoyable and interesting as possible for students and teachers alike. Over three years in the planning and compilation, it stands as a complete textbook in itself while acting as a companion volume to the highly regarded **Shin Nihongo no Kiso.**

As readers may know, **Shin Nihongo no Kiso** is a comprehensive introduction to elementary Japanese that serves as a highly efficient resource enabling students wishing to master basic Japanese conversation to do so in the shortest possible time. As such, although it was originally developed for use by AOTS's technical trainees, it is now used by a wide range of people both in Japan and abroad.

The teaching of Japanese is branching out in many different ways. Japanese economic and industrial growth has led to a greater level of interchange between Japan and other countries, and non-Japanese from a wide variety of backgrounds have come to Japan with a range of different objectives and are now living within local communities here. The changes in the social milieu surrounding the teaching of Japanese that have resulted from this influx of people from other countries have in turn influenced the individual situations in which Japanese is taught. There is now a greater diversity of learning needs, and they require individual responses.

It is against this background, and in response to the opinions and hopes expressed by a large number of people who have been involved in the teaching of Japanese for many years both in Japan and elsewhere, that 3A Corporation proudly publishes **Minna no Nihongo.** While the book continues to make use of the clarity and ease of understanding provided by the special features, key learning points and learning methods of **Shin Nihongo no Kiso**, the scenes, situations and characters in **Minna no Nihongo** have been made more universal in order to appeal to a wider range of learners. Its contents have been enhanced in this way to allow all kinds of students to use it for studying Japanese with pleasure.

Minna no Nihongo is aimed at anyone who urgently needs to learn to communicate in Japanese in any situation, whether at work, school, college or in their local community. Although it is an introductory text, efforts have been made to make the exchanges between Japanese and foreign characters in the book reflect Japanese social conditions and everyday life as faithfully as possible. While it is intended principally for those who have already left full-time education, it can also be recommended as an excellent textbook for university entrance courses as well as short-term intensive courses at technical colleges and universities.

We at 3A Corporation are continuing actively to produce new study materials designed to meet the individual needs of an increasingly wide range of learners, and we sincerely hope that readers will continue to give us their valued support.

In conclusion, I should like to mention the extensive help we received in the preparation of this text, in the form of suggestions and comments from various quarters and trials of the materials in actual lessons, for which we are extremely grateful. 3A Corporation intends to continue extending its network of friendship all over the world through activities such as the publishing of Japanese study materials, and we hope that everyone who knows us will continue to lend us their unstinting encouragement and support in this.

Iwao Ogawa
President, 3A Corporation
March 1998

EXPLANATORY NOTES

I. Structure

The learning materials consist of a Main Text, a Translation and Grammar Text and a set of cassette tapes/CDs. The Translation and Grammar Text is currently available in English. Versions in other languages will be published shortly.

The materials have been prepared with the main emphasis on listening and speaking Japanese; they do not provide instruction in reading and writing hiragana, katakana or kanji.

II. Content and Method of Use

1. Main Text

1) Japanese Pronunciation

This section gives examples of the main characteristics of Japanese pronunciation.

2) Classroom instructions, greetings, numerals

These are useful for understanding classroom instructions and daily greetings. They are frequently used by teachers in class.

3) Lessons

There are 25 lessons, and each contains the following:

① Sentence Patterns

Basic sentence patterns are shown in the order they appear.

② Example Sentences

A small dialogue in the style of a question and answer is given to show how the sentence patterns are used in practical conversation. New adverbs, conjunctions, and other grammatical points are also introduced.

③ Conversation

In the conversations, various foreign people staying in Japan appear in a variety of situations. The conversations include everyday expressions and greetings. As they are simple, learning them by heart is recommended. If time allows, students should try developing the conversation by applying the reference words given in each lesson of the Translation and Grammar Text in order to maximize their communication skills.

④ Drills

The drills are divided into three levels: A, B, and C.

Drill A is visually designed in chart style to help understanding of the grammatical structure. The style helps students to learn systematically the basic sentence patterns through substitution drills, and applying verb forms and conjugations following the chart.

Drill B has various drill patterns to strengthen students' grasp of the basic sentence patterns. Follow the directions given in each practice. Drills marked with a ☞ sign use pictorial charts.

Drill C is given in discourse style to show how the sentence patterns function in actual situations, and to enhance practical oral skills. Do not simply read, repeat and substitute, but try making your own substitution, enrich the content, and develop the story.

⑤ Practice

Two kinds of practices are given: one type for listening (👂) and the other for grammar practice.

The listening practice is further divided into a question asking for a personal answer, and a question confirming the key point of the given discourse. The listening practices are designed to strengthen students' aural skills, while the grammar practices check comprehension of vocabulary and the grammar points in the lessons studied.

The reading practices mostly require students to give a true or false response after reading a simple story compiled with words and sentence patterns from the lessons learned.

⑥ Review

This is provided to enable students to go over the essential points every several lessons studied.

⑦ Summary

At the end of the Main Text, a summary of grammatical points is given, such as the use of the particles, verb forms, adverbs and conjunctions, using example sentences appearing in the respective lessons.

⑧ Index

This includes classroom instructions, greetings, numerals, new vocabulary, and idiomatic expressions introduced in each lesson of the Main Text.

2. Translation and Grammar Text

1) Explanations of the general features and pronunciation of Japanese as well as the Japanese writing system

2) Translation of classroom instructions and greetings in the Main Text

3) The following are given in each of the 25 lessons.

① new vocabulary and its translation

② translation of Sentence Patterns, Example Sentences, and Conversation

③ useful words related to the lesson and small pieces of information on Japan and the Japanese

④ explanation of essential grammar appearing in the lesson

4) Translation of the particles, how to use the forms, adverbs and adverbial expressions, and various conjugations found at the back of the Main Text

5) Tables showing how to express numbers, time, periods of time, and counters, etc. including items which the textbook does not cover

3. Cassette Tapes/CDs

On the cassette tapes/CDs, Vocabulary, Sentence Patterns, Example Sentences, Drill C, Conversation and listening comprehension questions of the Practice section are recorded.

Students should pay attention to the pronunciation and intonation when listening to the Vocabulary, Sentence Patterns and Example Sentences. When listening to Drill C and Conversation, try to get accustomed to the natural speed of the language.

4. Kanji Usage

1) Kanji usage is based on 常用漢字表, which is an official list of the most commonly used Chinese characters in Japan.

① 熟字訓 (words which are made by a combination of two or more kanji and have a special reading) shown in the Appendix Chart of 常用漢字表

are written in kanji.

e.g. 友達(ともだち) friend　果物(くだもの) fruit　眼鏡(めがね) glasses

② Proper nouns are written with their own Chinese characters even if their readings are non-standard.

e.g. 大阪(おおさか) Osaka　奈良(なら) Nara　歌舞伎(かぶき) Kabuki

2) For freeing students from confusion, some words are given in kana although they are included in 常用漢字表(じょうようかんじひょう) and its Appendix Chart.

e.g. ある（有(あ)る possess・在(あ)る exist）　たぶん（多分(たぶん)）　perhaps
きのう（昨日(きのう)）　yesterday

3) Numbers are principally shown in Arabic numerals.

e.g. 9 時(じ) 9 o'clock　4 月(がつ)1 日(つ い た ち) 1st April　1 つ(ひと) one (thing)

However kanji is used in the following cases.

e.g. 一人(ひとり)で by oneself　一度(いちど) one time　一万円札(いちまんえんさつ) ten thousand yen bill

5. Miscellaneous

1) Words which can be omitted from a sentence are enclosed in square brackets [ ].

e.g. 父(ちち)は 54[歳(さい)]です。　My father is 54 years old.

2) Synonyms are enclosed in round brackets ( ).

e.g. だれ（どなた）　who

3) The part for an alternative word is denoted by ～.

e.g. ～は いかがですか。　How would you like ～?

If the alternative part is a numeral, － is used.

e.g. －歳(さい)　－ years old　－円(えん)　－ yen　－時間(じかん)　－ hours

TO USERS OF THIS TEXTBOOK
The most effective way to study

1. Learn each word carefully.
The *Translation & Grammatical Notes* introduces the new words for each lesson. First, listen to the tape/CD and learn these words thoroughly, paying special attention to the correct pronunciation and accent. Try to make sentences with the new words. It is important to memorize not only a word itself, but its use in a sentence.

2. Practice the sentence patterns.
Make sure you understand the meaning of each sentence pattern, and do *Drills A* and *B* until you have mastered the pattern. Say the sentences aloud, especially when doing *Drill B*.

3. Practice the conversation drills.
Sentence-pattern practice is followed by conversation practice. The example conversations show the various situations in actual daily life in which people from abroad will often need to use Japanese. Start by doing *Drill C* to get accustomed to the pattern. Don't practice only the dialogue pattern, but try to expand the dialogue. And learn how to communicate suitably according to the situations by practicing the conversation.

4. Listen to the cassette tape/CD repeatedly.
When practicing *Drill C* and *Conversation*, listen to the tape/CD and say the dialogue aloud to make sure you acquire the correct pronunciation and intonation. Listening to the tape/CD is the most effective way to get used to the sound and speed of Japanese and to improve your listening ability.

5. Always remember to review and prepare.
So as not to forget what you have learned in class, always review it the same day. Finally, do the questions at the end of each lesson in order to check what you have learnt and to test your listening comprehension. And, if you have time, look through the words and grammar explanation for the next lesson. Basic preparation is necessary for effective study.

6. Use what you have learnt.
Don't limit your learning to the classroom. Try to talk to Japanese people. Using what you have just learnt is the best way to progress.

If you complete this textbook following the above suggestions, you will have acquired the basic vocabulary and expressions necessary for daily life in Japan.

CHARACTERS IN THE CONVERSATIONS

Mike Miller

American, employee of IMC

Sato Keiko

Japanese, employee of IMC

Jose Santos

Brazilian, employee of Brazil Air

Maria Santos

Brazilian, housewife

Karina

Indonesian, student at Fuji University

Wang Xue

Chinese, doctor at Kobe Hospital

Yamada Ichiro

Japanese, employee of IMC

Yamada Tomoko

Japanese, bank clerk

Matsumoto Tadashi

Japanese,
department chief at IMC

Matsumoto Yoshiko

Japanese, housewife

Kimura Izumi

Japanese, announcer

—Other Characters—

Watt

British,
professor at Sakura University

Schmidt

German,
engineer at Power Electric Company

Lee

Korean,
research worker at AKC

Teresa

Brazilian, schoolgirl (9 yrs.),
daughter of Jose & Maria Santos

Taro

Japanese, schoolboy (8 yrs.),
son of Ichiro & Tomoko Yamada.

Gupta

Indian, employee of IMC

Thawaphon

Thai, student at Japanese language school

※**IMC** (computer software company)
※**AKC** (アジア研究センター: Asia Research Institute)

CONTENTS

I. Vocabulary   IV.Grammar Explanation

II. Translation   1. N_1は N_2です

   Sentence Patterns & Example Sentences   2. N_1は N_2じゃ ありません

   Conversation: 3. Sか

     How do you do?   4. Nも

III.Reference Words & Information: 5. N_1の N_2

   COUNTRY, PEOPLE & LANGUAGE   6. ～さん

I. Vocabulary   IV.Grammar Explanation

II. Translation   1. これ／それ／あれ

   Sentence Patterns & Example Sentences   2. この N／その N／あの N

   Conversation: 3. そうです／そうじゃ ありません

     This is just a token   4. S_1か、 S_2か

III.Reference Words & Information: 5. N_1の N_2

   FAMILY NAMES   6. そうですか

INTRODUCTION

I . General Features of Japanese

1. Parts of Speech

The Japanese language is comprised of verbs, adjectives, nouns, adverbs, conjunctions and particles.

2. Word Order

A predicate always comes at the end of a sentence. A modifier always comes before the word or phrase to be modified.

3. Predicate

There are three types of predicates in Japanese: noun, verb and adjective. A predicate inflects according to whether it is (1) affirmative or negative and (2) non-past or past.

Adjectives are divided into two types according to their type of inflection. They are called い-adjectives and な-adjectives.

In Japanese, words do not inflect for person, gender or number.

4. Particle

A particle is used to show the grammatical relation between words, to show the speaker's intention or to connect sentences.

5. Omission

Words or phrases are often omitted if they are understood from the context. Even the subject and object of a sentence are often omitted.

II . Japanese Script

There are three kinds of letters in Japanese: hiragana, katakana and kanji (Chinese characters). Hiragana and katakana are phonetic representations of sounds, and each letter basically corresponds to one mora (a unit of sound. See III). Kanji convey meanings as well as sounds.

In Japanese script, all three types of letters are used together. Katakana are used to write foreign names and loan words. 1945 kanji letters are fixed as essential for daily use. Hiragana are used to write particles, the inflectable parts of words, etc. Other than these three types of letters, romaji (Roman letters) are sometimes used for the convenience of foreigners. You may see romaji at stations and on sign-boards. Below are examples of all four types of script.

田中　さん　は　ミラー　さん　と　デパート　へ　行　きます。
○　　□　　□　△　　□　　□　　△　　□　○　□

Mr. Tanaka is going to the department store with Mr. Miller.

大阪　　Ｏ ｓ ａ ｋ ａ
○　　　☆

(○ − kanji　　□ − hiragana　　△ − katakana　　☆ − romaji)

III. Pronunciation of Japanese
1. Kana and Mora

e.g.,

| あ ア | hiragana script / katakana script |
| a | the Roman alphabet |

	あ-line	い-line	う-line	え-line	お-line
あ-row	あ ア a	い イ i	う ウ u	え エ e	お オ o
か-row k	か カ ka	き キ ki	く ク ku	け ケ ke	こ コ ko
さ-row s	さ サ sa	し シ shi	す ス su	せ セ se	そ ソ so
た-row t	た タ ta	ち チ chi	つ ツ tsu	て テ te	と ト to
な-row n	な ナ na	に ニ ni	ぬ ヌ nu	ね ネ ne	の ノ no
は-row h	は ハ ha	ひ ヒ hi	ふ フ fu	へ ヘ he	ほ ホ ho
ま-row m	ま マ ma	み ミ mi	む ム mu	め メ me	も モ mo
や-row y	や ヤ ya	(い イ) (i)	ゆ ユ yu	(え エ) (e)	よ ヨ yo
ら-row r	ら ラ ra	り リ ri	る ル ru	れ レ re	ろ ロ ro
わ-row w	わ ワ wa	(い イ) (i)	(う ウ) (u)	(え エ) (e)	を ヲ o
	ん ン n				

きゃ キャ kya	きゅ キュ kyu	きょ キョ kyo
しゃ シャ sha	しゅ シュ shu	しょ ショ sho
ちゃ チャ cha	ちゅ チュ chu	ちょ チョ cho
にゃ ニャ nya	にゅ ニュ nyu	にょ ニョ nyo
ひゃ ヒャ hya	ひゅ ヒュ hyu	ひょ ヒョ hyo
みゃ ミャ mya	みゅ ミュ myu	みょ ミョ myo

りゃ リャ rya	りゅ リュ ryu	りょ リョ ryo

	あ ア	い イ	う ウ	え エ	お オ
が-row g	が ガ ga	ぎ ギ gi	ぐ グ gu	げ ゲ ge	ご ゴ go
ざ-row z	ざ ザ za	じ ジ ji	ず ズ zu	ぜ ゼ ze	ぞ ゾ zo
だ-row d	だ ダ da	ぢ ヂ ji	づ ヅ zu	で デ de	ど ド do
ば-row b	ば バ ba	び ビ bi	ぶ ブ bu	べ ベ be	ぼ ボ bo
ぱ-row p	ぱ パ pa	ぴ ピ pi	ぷ プ pu	ぺ ペ pe	ぽ ポ po

ぎゃ ギャ gya	ぎゅ ギュ gyu	ぎょ ギョ gyo
じゃ ジャ ja	じゅ ジュ ju	じょ ジョ jo

びゃ ビャ bya	びゅ ビュ byu	びょ ビョ byo
ぴゃ ピャ pya	ぴゅ ピュ pyu	ぴょ ピョ pyo

The katakana letters in the square on the right are not in the above table. They are used to write sounds which are not original Japanese sounds but are needed for use in loan words.

	ウィ wi		ウェ we	ウォ wo
			シェ she	
			チェ che	
ツァ tsa			ツェ tse	ツォ tso
	ティ ti	トゥ tu		
ファ fa	フィ fi		フェ fe	フォ fo
			ジェ je	
	ディ di	ドゥ du		
	デュ dyu			

The Japanese language is based on five vowel sounds: あ (a), い (i), う (u), え (e) and お (o) (see the table on the previous page). All spoken sounds are derived from these five vowels. They are used alone or are attached to either a consonant (e.g., k + a = か) or a consonant plus the semi-vowel "y" (e.g., k + y + a = きゃ). The exception to this is a special mora, ん (n), which is not followed by vowels. All of these sounds are of equal length when spoken.

[Note 1] A mora is a unit of sound in Japanese.

[Note 2] In order to write the Japanese language according to the pronunciation, kana are used. (See "Kana and Mora" on the previous page.) One kana letter or one kana letter accompanied by a small kana letter (e.g., きゃ) basically corresponds to one mora.

2. Long Vowels

A long vowel is pronounced twice as long as the ordinary vowels あ, い, う, え and お. If you count the length of the vowel あ as one, the length of the long vowel ああ is counted as two. This means あ is one mora long, whereas ああ is two moras long.

Whether a vowel is long or not can change the meaning of the word.

e.g., おばさん (aunt) : おば<u>あ</u>さん (grandmother)
おじさん (uncle): おじ<u>い</u>さん (grandfather)
ゆき (snow) : ゆ<u>う</u>き (courage)
え (picture) : え<u>え</u> (yes)　とる (take): と<u>お</u>る (pass)
ここ (here): こ<u>う</u>こ<u>う</u> (high school)　へや(room): へ<u>い</u>や(plain)
カ<u>ー</u>ド (card)　タクシ<u>ー</u>(taxi)　ス<u>ー</u>パ<u>ー</u>(supermarket)
テ<u>ー</u>プ (tape)　ノ<u>ー</u>ト (notebook)

[Note]

1) How to write the long vowels in hiragana

(1) The long vowels of the あ-line
Add あ to the hiragana letters belonging to the あ-line.
(2) The long vowels of the い-line
Add い to the hiragana letters belonging to the い-line.
(3) The long vowels of the う-line
Add う to the hiragana letters belonging to the う-line.
(4) The long vowels of the え-line
Add い to the hiragana letters belonging to the え-line.
(exceptions: え<u>え</u> yes, ね<u>え</u> say, おね<u>え</u>さん elder sister)
(5) The long vowels of the お-line
Add う to the hiragana letters belonging to the お-line.
(exceptions: お<u>お</u>きい big, お<u>お</u>い many, と<u>お</u>い far, and some others)

4

2) How to write the long vowels in katakana

For all the lines, add "ー."

3. Pronunciation of ん

ん never appears at the beginning of a word. It constitutes one mora. For easier pronunciation, the way it is said changes according to the sound that comes after it.

1) It is pronounced /n/ before the sounds in the た-, だ-, ら- and な-rows.

   e.g., は<u>ん</u>たい (opposite)　う<u>ん</u>どう (sport)　せ<u>ん</u>ろ (rail)　み<u>ん</u>な (all)

2) It is pronounced /m/ before the sounds in the ば-, ぱ- and ま-rows.

   e.g., し<u>ん</u>ぶん (newspaper)　え<u>ん</u>ぴつ (pencil)　う<u>ん</u>めい (destiny)

3) It is pronounced /ŋ/ before the sounds in the か- and が-rows.

   e.g., て<u>ん</u>き (weather)　け<u>ん</u>がく (visit)

4. Pronunciation of っ

っ appears before a sound belonging to either the か-, さ-, た- or ぱ-row. In writing loan words, it is also used before sounds belonging to the ザ-row, ダ-row, etc. It constitutes one mora and has one mora's length.

   e.g.,　ぶか (subordinate) : ぶ<u>っ</u>か (commodity price)
   　　　かさい (fire) : か<u>っ</u>さい (applause)
   　　　おと (sound) : お<u>っ</u>と (husband)
   　　　に<u>っ</u>き (diary)　ざ<u>っ</u>し (magazine)　き<u>っ</u>て (stamp)
   　　　い<u>っ</u>ぱい (a cup of～)　コ<u>ッ</u>プ (glass)　ベ<u>ッ</u>ド (bed)

5. Pronunciation of Letters Combined with や, ゅ or ょ

き, ぎ, し, じ, ち, に, ひ, び, ぴ, み or り can combine with ゃ, ゅ or ょ, and the two letters together constitute one mora.

   e.g.,　ひやく (jump) : <u>ひゃ</u>く (hundred)
   　　　じゆう (freedom) : <u>じゅ</u>う (ten)
   　　　びよういん (beauty parlor) : <u>びょ</u>ういん (hospital)
   　　　<u>シャ</u>ツ (shirt)　お<u>ちゃ</u> (tea)　<u>ぎゅ</u>うにゅう (milk)
   　　　<u>きょ</u>う (today)　ぶ<u>ちょ</u>う (department chief)　<u>りょ</u>こう (travel)

6. Pronunciation of the が-row

The consonant of this row, when it comes at the beginning of a word, is pronounced [g]. In other cases, it is usually pronounced [ŋ]. Recently some Japanese do not differentiate between [g] and [ŋ], and always use [g].

7. Devoicing of Vowels [i] and [u]

The vowels [i] and [u] are devoiced and not heard when they come between voiceless consonants. The vowel [u] of す[su] in ～です or ～ます is also devoiced when the sentence finishes with either ～です or ～ます.

e.g., すき (like)   したいです (want to do)   ききます (listen)

8. Accent

The Japanese language has pitch accent. That is, some moras in a word are pronounced high and others low. The words are divided into two types according to whether a word has a falling pitch or not. Words with a falling pitch are subdivided into three types according to where the fall in pitch occurs. The standard Japanese accent is characterized by the fact that the first and the second moras have different pitches, and that the pitch never rises again once it has fallen.

[Types of Accent]

1) A fall in pitch does not occur.   【 ＿￣ 】
   e.g., にわ (garden) はな (nose) なまえ (name) にほんご(Japanese language)

2) A fall in pitch comes after the first mora.   【 ￣＿ 】
   e.g., ほん (book)   てんき (weather)   らいげつ (next month)

3) A fall in pitch comes in the word at some place after the second mora.   【 ＿￣＿ 】
   e.g., たまご (egg)   ひこうき (airplane)   せんせい (teacher)

4) A fall in pitch comes after the last mora.   【 ＿￣】
   e.g., くつ(shoes) はな(flower) やすみ(holiday) おとうと(younger brother)

"はな (nose)" in 1) and "はな (flower)" in 4) are alike, but the type of accent is different, because if a particle like が is added after each word 1) is pronounced はなが, whereas 4) is pronounced はなが. The following are some other examples of words whose meaning differ according to the type of accent.

e.g., はし(bridge) : はし (chopsticks)   いち(one) : いち (location)

There are local differences in accent. For example, the accent of the area around Osaka is quite different from the standard one. The following are examples.

e.g.,   Tokyo accent   :   Osaka accent
          (standard Japanese accent)
                              はな   :   はな   (flower)
                              りんご   :   りんご   (apple)
                          おんがく   :   おんがく   (music)

9. Intonation

There are three patterns. They are 1) flat, 2) rising and 3) falling. Questions are pronounced with a rising intonation. Other sentences are usually pronounced flat, but sometimes with a falling intonation. A falling intonation can express feelings such as agreement or disappointment, etc.

e.g.,　佐藤　：あした 友達と お花見を します。【→ flat】

　　　　　　　ミラーさんも いっしょに 行きませんか。【↗rising】

　　　　ミラー：ああ、いいですねえ。　【↘ falling】

　　　　Sato　　：I'll go to see the cherry blossoms with my friends tomorrow.

　　　　　　　　　Won't you come with us, Mr. Miller?

　　　　Miller　：Oh, that sounds good.

PRELIMINARY LESSON

I . Pronunciation

1. Kana and Mora

2. Long Vowels
おばさん (aunt) : おば<u>あ</u>さん (grandmother)
おじさん (uncle) : おじ<u>い</u>さん (grandfather)
ゆき (snow) : ゆ<u>う</u>き (courage)
え (picture) : え<u>え</u> (yes)
とる (take) : と<u>お</u>る (pass)
ここ (here) : こ<u>う</u>こ<u>う</u> (high school)　へや (room) : へ<u>い</u>や (plain)
カ<u>ー</u>ド (card)　タクシ<u>ー</u> (taxi)　ス<u>ー</u>パ<u>ー</u> (supermarket)
テ<u>ー</u>プ (tape)　ノ<u>ー</u>ト (notebook)

3. Pronunciation of ん
え<u>ん</u>ぴつ (pencil)　み<u>ん</u>な (all)　て<u>ん</u>き (weather)　き<u>ん</u>え<u>ん</u> (no smoking)

4. Pronunciation of っ
ぶか (subordinate) : ぶ<u>っ</u>か (commodity price)
かさい (fire) : か<u>っ</u>さい (applause)
おと (sound) : お<u>っ</u>と (husband)
に<u>っ</u>き (diary)　ざ<u>っ</u>し (magazine)　き<u>っ</u>て (stamp)
い<u>っ</u>ぱい (a cup of 〜)　コ<u>ッ</u>プ (glass)　ベ<u>ッ</u>ド (bed)

5. Pronunciation of Letters Combined with や, ゅ or ょ
ひやく (jump) : <u>ひゃ</u>く (hundred)
じゆう (freedom) : <u>じゅ</u>う (ten)
びよういん (beauty parlor) : <u>びょ</u>ういん (hospital)
<u>シャ</u>ツ (shirt)　お<u>ちゃ</u> (tea)　<u>ぎゅ</u>うに<u>ゅ</u>う (milk)
<u>きょ</u>う (today)　ぶ<u>ちょ</u>う (department chief)　<u>りょ</u>こう (travel)

6. Accent
に<u>わ</u> (garden)　な<u>まえ</u> (name)　に<u>ほんご</u> (Japanese language)　【￢】
<u>ほ</u>ん (book)　て<u>ん</u>き (weather)　ら<u>いげ</u>つ (next month)　【￣￢】
た<u>ま</u>ご (egg)　ひ<u>こ</u>うき (airplane)　せ<u>んせ</u>い (teacher)　【￣￣￢】
<u>く</u>つ (shoes)　や<u>すみ</u> (holiday)　お<u>とうと</u> (younger brother)　【￣￣￣】
は<u>し</u> (bridge) : は<u>し</u> (chopsticks)　い<u>ち</u> (one) : い<u>ち</u> (location)

	Tokyo accent	:	Osaka accent	
	は<u>な</u>	:	<u>は</u>な	(flower)
	<u>りんご</u>	:	<u>り</u>んご	(apple)
	<u>お</u>んがく	:	お<u>ん</u>がく	(music)

7. Intonation

e.g., 佐藤<ruby>さとう</ruby> ：あした 友達<ruby>ともだち</ruby>と お花見<ruby>はなみ</ruby>を します。【→】

　　　　　　　ミラーさんも いっしょに 行きませんか。【↗】

　　ミラー ：ああ、いいですねえ。　【↘】

　　Sato　　：I'll go to see the cherry blossoms with my friends tomorrow.

　　　　　　　Won't you come with us, Mr. Miller?

　　Miller　：Oh, that sounds good.

II. Classroom Instructions

1. Let's begin.
2. Let's finish (the lesson).
3. Let's take a break.
4. Do you understand? (Yes, I do./No, I don't.)
5. Once more.
6. Fine. / Good.
7. That's not OK. / That's wrong.
8. name
9. exam, homework
10. question, answer, example

III. Daily Greetings and Expressions

1. Good morning.
2. Good afternoon.
3. Good evening.
4. Good night.
5. Good-bye.
6. Thank you very much.
7. Excuse me. / I'm sorry.
8. Please.

IV. Numerals

0	zero
1	one
2	two
3	three
4	four
5	five
6	six
7	seven
8	eight
9	nine
10	ten

TERMS USED FOR INSTRUCTION

第一課	lesson －	名詞	noun
文型	sentence pattern	動詞	verb
例文	example sentence	形容詞	adjective
会話	conversation	い形容詞	い-adjective
練習	practice	な形容詞	な-adjective
問題	exercise	助詞	particle
答え	answer	副詞	advcrb
読み物	reading practice	接続詞	conjunction
復習	review	数詞	quantifier
		助数詞	counters
目次	contents	疑問詞	interrogative
			(question word)
索引	index		
		名詞文	noun (predicate) sentence
文法	grammar	動詞文	verb (predicate) sentence
文	sentence	形容詞文	adjective (predicate) sentence
単語（語）	word		
句	phrase	主語	subject
節	clause	述語	predicate
		目的語	object
発音	pronunciation	主題	topic
母音	vowel		
子音	consonant	肯定	affirmative
拍	mora	否定	negative
アクセント	accent	完了	perfective
イントネーション	intonation	未完了	imperfective
		過去	past
[か]行	[か]row	非過去	non-past
[い]列	[い]line		
丁寧体	polite style of speech		
普通体	plain style of speech		
活用	inflection		
フォーム	form		
～形	～form		
修飾	modification		
例外	exception		

ABBREVIATIONS

N   noun （名詞）

                 e.g.   がくせい   つくえ

                          student   desk

い-adj   い-adjective （い形容詞）

                 e.g.   おいしい   たかい

                          tasty   high

な-adj   な-adjective （な形容詞）

                 e.g.   きれい[な]   しずか[な]

                          beautiful   quiet

V   verb （動詞）

                 e.g.   かきます   たべます

                          write   eat

S   sentence （文）

                 e.g.   これは 本です。

                       This is a book.

                   わたしは あした 東京へ 行きます。

                       I will go to Tokyo tomorrow.

Lesson 1

I. Vocabulary

わたし		I
わたしたち		we
あなた		you
あの ひと	あの 人	that person, he, she
（あの かた）	（あの 方）	（あの かた is the polite equivalent of あの ひと）
みなさん	皆さん	ladies and gentlemen, all of you
～さん		Mr., Ms. (title of respect added to a name)
～ちゃん		(suffix often added to a child's name instead of ～さん)
～くん	～君	(suffix often added to a boy's name)
～じん	～人	(suffix meaning "a national of"; e.g., アメリカじん, an American)
せんせい	先生	teacher, instructor (not used when referring to one's own job)
きょうし	教師	teacher, instructor
がくせい	学生	student
かいしゃいん	会社員	company employee
しゃいん	社員	employee of ～ Company (used with a company's name; e.g., IMCの しゃいん)
ぎんこういん	銀行員	bank employee
いしゃ	医者	medical doctor
けんきゅうしゃ	研究者	researcher, scholar
エンジニア		engineer
だいがく	大学	university
びょういん	病院	hospital
でんき	電気	electricity, light
だれ（どなた）		who (どなた is the polite equivalent of だれ)

－さい	－歳	－ years old
なんさい	何歳	how old（おいくつ is the polite equivalent
（おいくつ）		of なんさい）
はい		yes
いいえ		no

しつれいですが	失礼ですが	Excuse me, but
おなまえは？	お名前は？	May I have your name?
はじめまして。	初めまして。	How do you do? (lit. I am meeting you for the first time. Usually used as the first phrase when introducing oneself.)
どうぞ よろしく ［おねがいします］。		Pleased to meet you. (lit. Please be nice
どうぞ よろしく ［お願いします］。		to me. Usually used at the end of a self-introduction.)
こちらは ～さんです。		This is Mr./Ms.～.
～から きました。		I came (come) from ～.
～から 来ました。		

〰〰〰〰〰〰〰〰〰〰〰〰〰〰〰〰〰〰〰〰

アメリカ	U.S.A.
イギリス	U.K.
インド	India
インドネシア	Indonesia
韓国	South Korea
タイ	Thailand
中国	China
ドイツ	Germany
日本	Japan
フランス	France
ブラジル	Brazil
さくら大学／富士大学	fictitious universities
ＩＭＣ／パワー電気／ブラジルエアー	
	fictitious companies
ＡＫＣ	fictitious institute
神戸病院	fictitious hospital

II. Translation

Sentence Patterns

1. I am Mike Miller.
2. Mr. Santos is not a student.
3. Is Mr. Miller a company employee?
4. Mr. Santos is also a company employee.

Example Sentences

1. Are you Mr. Mike Miller?
   ···Yes, I am Mike Miller.

2. Are you a student, Mr. Miller?
   ···No, I am not a student.
   I am a company employee.

3. Is Mr. Wang an engineer?
   ···No, Mr. Wang is not an engineer.
   He is a doctor.

4. Who is that person?
   ···He is Professor Watt. He is a teacher at Sakura University.

5. How old is Teresa?
   ···She is nine years old.

Conversation

How do you do?

Sato:	Good morning.
Yamada:	Good morning.
	Ms. Sato, this is Mr. Mike Miller.
Miller:	How do you do? I am Mike Miller.
	I am from the United States of America.
	Nice to meet you.
Sato:	I am Sato Keiko.
	Nice to meet you.

III. Reference Words & Information

国・人・ことば　　COUNTRY, PEOPLE & LANGUAGE

国　Country	人　People	ことば　Language
アメリカ (U.S.A.)	アメリカ人	英語 (English)
イギリス (U.K.)	イギリス人	英語 (English)
イタリア (Italy)	イタリア人	イタリア語 (Italian)
イラン (Iran)	イラン人	ペルシア語 (Persian)
インド (India)	インド人	ヒンディー語 (Hindi)
インドネシア (Indonesia)	インドネシア人	インドネシア語 (Indonesian)
エジプト (Egypt)	エジプト人	アラビア語 (Arabic)
オーストラリア(Australia)	オーストラリア人	英語 (English)
カナダ (Canada)	カナダ人	英語 (English) フランス語 (French)
韓国 (South Korea)	韓国人	韓国語 (Korean)
サウジアラビア(Saudi Arabia)	サウジアラビア人	アラビア語 (Arabic)
シンガポール (Singapore)	シンガポール人	英語 (English)
スペイン (Spain)	スペイン人	スペイン語 (Spanish)
タイ (Thailand)	タイ人	タイ語 (Thai)
中国 (China)	中国人	中国語 (Chinese)
ドイツ (Germany)	ドイツ人	ドイツ語 (German)
日本 (Japan)	日本人	日本語 (Japanese)
フランス (France)	フランス人	フランス語 (French)
フィリピン (Philippines)	フィリピン人	フィリピノ語 (Filipino)
ブラジル (Brazil)	ブラジル人	ポルトガル語 (Portuguese)
ベトナム (Vietnam)	ベトナム人	ベトナム語 (Vietnamese)
マレーシア (Malaysia)	マレーシア人	マレーシア語 (Malaysian)
メキシコ (Mexico)	メキシコ人	スペイン語 (Spanish)
ロシア (Russia)	ロシア人	ロシア語 (Russian)

IV. Grammar Explanation

1. │ N₁ は N₂ です │

1) Particle は

The particle は indicates that the word before it is the topic of the sentence. You select a noun you want to talk about, add は to show that it is the topic and give a statement about the topic.

　　① わたしは マイク・ミラーです。　　　　I am Mike Miller.

[Note] The particle は is read わ.

2) です

Nouns used with です work as predicates.
です indicates judgement or assertion.
です also conveys that the speaker is being polite towards the listener.
です inflects when the sentence is negative (see 2. below) or in the past tense (see Lesson 12).

　　② わたしは エンジニアです。　　　　　I am an engineer.

2. │ N₁ は N₂ じゃ ありません │

じゃ ありません is the negative form of です. It is the form used in daily conversation. For a formal speech or writing, では ありません is used instead.

　　③ サントスさんは 学生じゃ ありません。　Mr. Santos is not a student.
　　　　　　　　　　（では）

[Note] は in では is read わ.

3. │ S か │

1) Particle か

The particle か is used to express the speaker's doubt, question, uncertainty, etc. A question is formed by simply adding か to the end of the sentence. A question ends with a rising intonation.

2) Questions asking whether a statement is correct or not

As mentioned above, a sentence becomes a question when か is added to the end. The word order does not change. The question thus made asks whether a statement is correct or not. Depending on whether you agree with the statement or not, your answer to such a question begins with はい or いいえ.

　　④ ミラーさんは アメリカ人ですか。　　　Is Mr. Miller an American?
　　　　…はい、アメリカ人です。　　　　　　…Yes, he is.
　　⑤ ミラーさんは 先生ですか。　　　　　　Is Mr. Miller a teacher?
　　　　…いいえ、先生じゃ ありません。　　　…No, he is not.

3) Questions with interrogatives

An interrogative replaces the part of the sentence that covers what you want to ask about. The word order does not change, and か is added at the end.

　　⑥ あの 方は どなたですか。　　　　　　Who is that man?
　　　　… [あの 方は] ミラーさんです。　　　…That's Mr. Miller.

4. N も

も is added after a topic instead of は when the statement about the topic is the same as the previous topic.

⑦ ミラーさんは 会社員です。　　Mr. Miller is a company employee.
　グプタさんも 会社員です。　　Mr. Gupta is also a company employee.

5. N₁ の N₂

の is used to connect two nouns. N₁ modifies N₂. In Lesson 1, N₁ is an organization or some kind of group to which N₂ belongs.

⑧ ミラーさんは ＩＭＣの 社員です。　Mr. Miller is an IMC employee.

6. ～さん

さん is added to the name of the listener or a third person to show the speaker's respect to the person. It should never be used with the speaker's own name.

⑨ あの 方は ミラーさんです。　　That's Mr. Miller.

When referring directly to the listener, the word あなた (you) is not commonly used if you know the listener's name. The listener's family name followed by さん is usually used.

⑩ 鈴木：　ミラーさんは 学生ですか。
　ミラー：いいえ、会社員です。
　Suzuki：　Are you a student?
　Miller：　No, I'm a company employee.

Lesson 2

I. Vocabulary

これ		this (thing here)
それ		that (thing near you)
あれ		that (thing over there)
この ～		this ～, this ～ here
その ～		that ～, that ～ near you
あの ～		that ～, that ～ over there
ほん	本	book
じしょ	辞書	dictionary
ざっし	雑誌	magazine
しんぶん	新聞	newspaper
ノート		notebook
てちょう	手帳	pocket notebook
めいし	名刺	business card
カード		card
テレホンカード		telephone card
えんぴつ	鉛筆	pencil
ボールペン		ballpoint pen
シャープペンシル		mechanical pencil, propelling pencil
かぎ		key
とけい	時計	watch, clock
かさ	傘	umbrella
かばん		bag, briefcase
[カセット]テープ		[cassette] tape
テープレコーダー		tape recorder
テレビ		television
ラジオ		radio
カメラ		camera
コンピューター		computer
じどうしゃ	自動車	automobile, car

つくえ	机	desk
いす		chair
チョコレート		chocolate
コーヒー		coffee
えいご	英語	the English language
にほんご	日本語	the Japanese language
〜ご	〜語	〜 language
なん	何	what
そう		so

ちがいます。	違います。	No, it isn't./You are wrong.
そうですか。		I see./Is that so?
あのう		well (used to show hesitation)
ほんの きもちです。		It's nothing./It's a token of my gratitude.
ほんの 気持ちです。		
どうぞ。		Please./Here you are. (used when offering someone something)
どうも。		Well, thanks.
［どうも］ ありがとう ［ございます］。		Thank you [very much].

◁会話▷
これから お世話に なります。	I hope for your kind assistance hereafter.
こちらこそ よろしく。	I am pleased to meet you. (response to どうぞ よろしく)

II. Translation

Sentence Patterns

1. This is a dictionary.
2. This is a book on computers.
3. That is my umbrella.
4. This umbrella is mine.

Example Sentences

1. Is this a telephone card?
   ···Yes, it is.

2. Is that a notebook?
   ···No, it's not. It's a pocket notebook.

3. What is that?
   ···This is a business card.

4. Is this a "9" or a "7"?
   ···It's a "9."

5. What is that magazine about?
   ···It's a magazine on cars.

6. Whose bag is that?
   ···It's Ms. Sato's bag.

7. Is this umbrella yours?
   ···No, it's not mine.

8. Whose is this key?
   ···It's mine.

Conversation

This is just a token

Yamada:	Yes. Who is it?
Santos:	I am Santos from (apartment) 408.

Santos:	Hello. I am Santos.
	How do you do?
	It is nice to meet you.
Yamada:	The pleasure's mine.
Santos:	Er, this is a little something...
Yamada:	Oh, thank you. What is it?
Santos:	It's coffee. Please.
Yamada:	Thank you very much.

III. Reference Words & Information

名前　FAMILY NAMES
（なまえ）

Most Common Family Names

1	佐藤	2	鈴木	3	高橋	4	田中
5	渡辺	6	伊藤	7	中村	8	山本
9	小林	10	斎藤	11	加藤	12	吉田
13	山田	14	佐々木	15	松本	16	山口
17	木村	18	井上	19	阿部	20	林

Greetings

初めまして。
（はじ）

⇦ When people meet for the first time on business, business cards are exchanged.

ほんの 気持ちです。
（き も）

When you move house, it is polite to introduce yourself to your new neighbours and give them a small gift, such as a towel, soap or sweets. ⇨

IV. Grammar Explanation

1. これ／それ／あれ

これ, それ and あれ are demonstratives.

    They work as nouns. これ refers to a thing near the speaker. それ refers to a thing near the listener. あれ refers to a thing far from the speaker and the listener.

    ① それは 辞書ですか。   Is that a dictionary?

    ② これを ください。   I'll take this. (lit. Please give this to me.)(L. 3)

2. この N／その N／あの N

この, その and あの modify nouns. "この N" refers to a thing or a person near the speaker. "その N" refers to a thing or a person near the listener. "あの N" refers to a thing or a person far from both the speaker and the listener.

    ③ この 本は わたしのです。   This book is mine.

    ④ あの 方は どなたですか。   Who is that [person]?

3. そうです／そうじゃ ありません

In the case of a noun sentence, the word そう is often used to answer a question requiring an affirmative or negative answer. はい、そうです is the affirmative answer and いいえ、そうじゃ ありません is the negative answer.

    ⑤ それは テレホンカードですか。   Is that a telephone card?

      …はい、そうです。   …Yes, it is. (lit. Yes, it's so.)

    ⑥ それは テレホンカードですか。   Is that a telephone card?

      …いいえ、そうじゃ ありません。 …No, it isn't. (lit. No, it's not so.)

The verb ちがいます (lit. to differ) can be used to mean そうじゃ ありません.

    ⑦ それは テレホンカードですか。   Is that a telephone card?

      …いいえ、違います。   …No, it isn't.

4. $\boxed{\text{S}_1 \text{ か、 S}_2 \text{ か}}$

This is a question asking the listener to choose between alternatives, S_1 and S_2, for the answer. As an answer to this type of question, the chosen sentence is stated. Neither はい nor いいえ is used.

⑧ これは 「9」ですか、「7」ですか。　Is this a "9" or a "7"?
　…「9」です。　　　　　　　　　　　　…It's a "9."

5. $\boxed{\text{N}_1 \text{ の N}_2}$

You learned in Lesson 1 that の is used to connect two nouns when N_1 modifies N_2. In Lesson 2 you learn two other uses of this の.

1) N_1 explains what N_2 is about.

⑨ これは コンピューターの 本です。　This is a book on computers.

2) N_1 explains who owns N_2.

⑩ これは わたしの 本です。　This is my book.

N_2 is sometimes omitted when it is obvious. When N_2 means a person, however, you cannot omit it.

⑪ あれは だれの かばんですか。　Whose bag is that?
　…佐藤さんのです。　　　　　　　　　…It's Ms. Sato's.

⑫ この かばんは あなたのですか。　Is this bag yours?
　…いいえ、わたしのじゃ ありません。　…No, it's not mine.

⑬ ミラーさんは ＩＭＣの 社員ですか。
　…はい、ＩＭＣの 社員です。
　Is Mr. Miller an employee of IMC?
　…Yes, he is.

6.　そうですか

This expression is used when the speaker receives new information and shows that he or she understands it.

⑭ この 傘は あなたのですか。
　…いいえ、違います。シュミットさんのです。
　そうですか。
　Is this umbrella yours?
　…No, it's Mr. Schmidt's.
　I see.

Lesson 3

I. Vocabulary

ここ		here, this place
そこ		there, that place near you
あそこ		that place over there
どこ		where, what place
こちら		this way, this place (polite equivalent of ここ)
そちら		that way, that place near you (polite equivalent of そこ)
あちら		that way, that place over there (polite equivalent of あそこ)
どちら		which way, where (polite equivalent of どこ)
きょうしつ	教室	classroom
しょくどう	食堂	dining hall, canteen
じむしょ	事務所	office
かいぎしつ	会議室	conference room, assembly room
うけつけ	受付	reception desk
ロビー		lobby
へや	部屋	room
トイレ(おてあらい)	(お手洗い)	toilet, rest room
かいだん	階段	staircase
エレベーター		elevator, lift
エスカレーター		escalator
[お]くに	[お]国	country
かいしゃ	会社	company
うち		house, home
でんわ	電話	telephone, telephone call
くつ	靴	shoes
ネクタイ		necktie
ワイン		wine
たばこ		tobacco, cigarette
うりば	売り場	department, counter (in a department store)

ちか	地下	basement
ーかい（ーがい）	ー階	-th floor
なんがい	何階	what floor
ーえん	ー円	ー yen
いくら		how much
ひゃく	百	hundred
せん	千	thousand
まん	万	ten thousand

◁会話▷

すみません。	Excuse me.
〜でございます。	(polite equivalent of です)
［〜を］見せて ください。	Please show me ［〜］.
じゃ	well, then, in that case
［〜を］ください。	Give me ［〜］, please.

〰〰〰〰〰〰〰〰〰〰〰〰〰〰〰〰〰〰

新大阪	name of a station in Osaka
イタリア	Italy
スイス	Switzerland
ＭＴ／ヨーネン／アキックス	fictitious companies

3

II. Translation

Sentence Patterns

1. This is a dining hall.
2. The telephone is over there.

Example Sentences

1. Is this Shin-Osaka?
   ···Yes, it is.

2. Where is the rest room?
   ···It is over there.

3. Where is Mr. Yamada?
   ···He is in the office.

4. Where is the elevator?
   ···It is there.

5. Which country are you from?
   ···America.

6. Where are those shoes from?
   ···They're Italian shoes.

7. How much is this watch?
   ···It's 18,600 yen.

Conversation

I'll take it

Maria:	Excuse me. Where is the wine department?
Sales clerk A:	It is in the first basement.
Maria:	Thanks.

Maria:	Excuse me. Could you show me that wine?
Sales clerk B:	Certainly. Here you are.
Maria:	Is this French wine?
Sales clerk B:	No, it's Italian.
Maria:	How much is it?
Sales clerk B:	2,500 yen.
Maria:	Well, I'll take it.

III. Reference Words & Information

デパート　　DEPARTMENT STORE

屋上	遊園地 amusement area
8階	食堂・催し物会場 restaurants・event hall
7階	時計・眼鏡・カメラ watches・glasses・cameras
6階	スポーツ用品・旅行用品 sporting goods・leisure goods
5階	子ども服・おもちゃ・本・文房具 children's clothes・toys・books・stationery
4階	家具・食器・電気製品 furniture・kitchenware・electrical appliances
3階	紳士服 men's wear
2階	婦人服 ladies' wear
1階	靴・かばん・アクセサリー・化粧品 shoes・bags・accessories・cosmetics
B1階	食料品 food
B2階	駐車場 parking lot

IV. Grammar Explanation

1. ここ／そこ／あそこ／こちら／そちら／あちら

The demonstratives これ, それ and あれ that are discussed in Lesson 2 refer to a thing, while ここ, そこ and あそこ refer to a place. ここ is the place where the speaker is, そこ is the place where the listener is, and あそこ is the place far from both the speaker and the listener.

こちら, そちら and あちら are demonstrative words referring to direction. こちら, そちら and あちら are also used to refer to location, in which case, they are politer than ここ, そこ and あそこ.

[Note] When the speaker regards the listener as sharing his/her territory, the place where they both are is designated by the word ここ. Under this situation, そこ designates the place a little distant from the speaker and listener, and あそこ designates an even more distant location.

2. N₁ は N₂(place)です

Using this sentence pattern, you can explain where a place, a thing or a person is.

① お手洗いは あそこです。　　　The rest room is there.
② 電話は 2階です。　　　The telephone is on the second floor.
③ 山田さんは 事務所です。　　　Mr. Yamada is in the office.

3. どこ／どちら

どこ means "where," and どちら means "which direction." どちら can also mean "where," in which case it's politer than どこ.

④ お手洗いは どこですか。　　　Where's the rest room?
　…あそこです。　　　…It's there.
⑤ エレベーターは どちらですか。　Where's the elevator?
　…あちらです。　　　…It's in that direction. (It's there.)

どこ or どちら is also used to ask the name of a country, company, school or any place or organization a person belongs to. You cannot use なん(what). どちら is politer than どこ.

⑥ 学校は どこですか。　　　　　　What's the name of your school?

⑦ 会社は どちらですか。　　　　　What company do you work for?

4. N₁ の N₂

When N₁ is the name of a country and N₂ is a product, it means that N₂ is made in that country. When N₁ is the name of a company and N₂ is a product, it means that N₂ is made by that company. In this structure, どこ is used to ask where or by whom N₂ is made.

⑧ これは どこの コンピューターですか。

…日本の コンピューターです。

…IMCの コンピューターです。

Where is this computer made?/ Who is the maker of this computer?

…It's made in Japan.

…IMC is.

5. The こ／そ／あ／ど system of demonstrative words

	こ series	そ series	あ series	ど series
thing	これ	それ	あれ	どれ (L. 8)
thing person	この N	その N	あの N	どの N (L. 16)
place	ここ	そこ	あそこ	どこ
direction place (polite)	こちら	そちら	あちら	どちら

6. お国

The prefix お is added to a word concerning the listener or a third person in order to express the speaker's respect to the person.

⑨ ［お］国は どちらですか。　　　　Where are you from?

Lesson 4

I.　Vocabulary

おきます	起きます	get up, wake up
ねます	寝ます	sleep, go to bed
はたらきます	働きます	work
やすみます	休みます	take a rest, take a holiday
べんきょうします	勉強します	study
おわります	終わります	finish
デパート		department store
ぎんこう	銀行	bank
ゆうびんきょく	郵便局	post office
としょかん	図書館	library
びじゅつかん	美術館	art museum
いま	今	now
ーじ	一時	ー o'clock
ーふん（ーぷん）	一分	ー minute
はん	半	half
なんじ	何時	what time
なんぷん	何分	what minute
ごぜん	午前	a.m., morning
ごご	午後	p.m., afternoon
あさ	朝	morning
ひる	昼	daytime, noon
ばん（よる）	晩（夜）	night, evening
おととい		the day before yesterday
きのう		yesterday
きょう		today
あした		tomorrow
あさって		the day after tomorrow
けさ		this morning
こんばん	今晩	this evening, tonight
やすみ	休み	rest, a holiday, a day off
ひるやすみ	昼休み	lunchtime

まいあさ	毎朝	every morning
まいばん	毎晩	every night
まいにち	毎日	every day
げつようび	月曜日	Monday
かようび	火曜日	Tuesday
すいようび	水曜日	Wednesday
もくようび	木曜日	Thursday
きんようび	金曜日	Friday
どようび	土曜日	Saturday
にちようび	日曜日	Sunday
なんようび	何曜日	what day of the week
ばんごう	番号	number
なんばん	何番	what number
～から		from ～
～まで		up to ～, until ～
～と～		and (used to connect nouns)
そちら		your place
たいへんですね。	大変ですね。	That's tough, isn't it? (used when expressing sympathy)
えーと		well, let me see

◁会話▷

１０４	information, directory assistance
お願いします。	Please. (lit. ask for a favor)
かしこまりました。	Certainly (sir, madam).
お問い合わせの番号	the number being inquired about
［どうも］ありがとう ございました。	Thank you very much.

~~~~~~~~~~~~~~~~~~~~~~~~~~~~

ニューヨーク	New York
ペキン	Beijing (北京)
ロンドン	London
バンコク	Bangkok
ロサンゼルス	Los Angeles
やまと美術館	fictitious art museum
大阪デパート	fictitious department store
みどり図書館	fictitious library
アップル銀行	fictitious bank

II. Translation

Sentence Patterns

1. It is five past four now.
2. I work from nine to five.
3. I get up at six in the morning.
4. I studied yesterday.

Example Sentences

1. What time is it now?
   ···It is ten past two.
   What time is it now in New York?
   ···It is ten past twelve at night.

2. From what time to what time is the bank open?
   ···It is open from nine till three.
   On what day of the week is it closed?
   ···It is closed on Saturdays and Sundays.

3. What time do you go to bed every night?
   ···I go to bed at eleven o'clock.

4. Do you work on Saturdays?
   ···No, I don't.

5. Did you study yesterday?
   ···No, I didn't.

6. What is the telephone number of IMC?
   ···It is 341-2597.

Conversation

What are your opening hours?

104:	Hello, this is Ishida of the 104 Service.
Karina:	Could you tell me the phone number of the Yamato Art Museum, please?
104:	The Yamato Art Museum? Certainly.

Tape:	The number you are inquiring about is 0797-38-5432.

Museum staff member:	Hello, Yamato Art Museum.
Karina:	Excuse me. What are your opening hours?
Staff:	We are open from nine to four.
Karina:	Which day of the week are you closed?
Staff:	We are closed on Mondays.
Karina:	Thank you very much.

III. Reference Words & Information

電話・手紙　PHONE & LETTER

 How to Use a Public Phone

① Lift the receiver.　② Put coin or card into slot.　③ Press the numbers.　④ Hang up the receiver.　⑤ Take card or change if any.

Public phones accept only ¥10 coins, ¥100 coins, and telephone cards.
If you put in a ¥100 coin, no change will be returned.
* If the machine has a start button, press it after ③.

 Emergency Numbers and Others

1 1 0	警察署	police
1 1 9	消防署	fire/ambulance
1 1 7	時報	time
1 7 7	天気予報	weather forecast
1 0 4	電話番号案内	directory assistance services

 How to Write an Address

district　postal zip code　city　ward　town

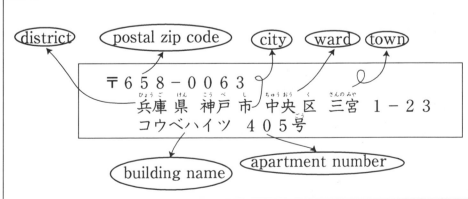

〒658-0063
兵庫県 神戸市 中央区 三宮 1-23
コウベハイツ 405号

building name　apartment number

IV. Grammar Explanation

1. | 今 －時－分です |

To express time, the counter suffixes 時 (o'clock) and 分 (minutes) are used. The numbers are put before them. 分 is read ふん after 2, 5, 7 or 9 and ぷん after 1, 3, 4, 6, 8 or 10. 1, 6, 8 and 10 are read いっ, ろっ, はっ and じゅっ (じっ) before ぷん. (See Appendices II.)

The interrogative なん is used with a counter suffix to ask questions concerning number or amounts. Therefore, the word なんじ (or sometimes なんぷん) is used to ask the time.

① 今 何時ですか。　　　　　　What time is it now?
　…7時10分です。　　　　　…It's seven ten.

[Note] は marks the topic of a sentence, which you learned in Lesson 1. A geographical location can also be used as the topic as can be seen in ②.

② ニューヨークは 今 何時ですか。In New York what time is it now?
　…午前 4時です。　　　　　…It's 4 a.m.

2. | V ます |

1) A verb with ます works as a predicate.
2) ます makes a sentence polite.

③ わたしは 毎日 勉強します。　　I study every day.

3. | V ます／V ません／V ました／V ませんでした |

1) ます is used when a sentence expresses a habitual thing or a truth. It is also used when a sentence expresses a thing that will occur in the future. The negative form and the forms in the past tense are shown in the table below.

	non-past (future/present)	past
affirmative	（おき）ます	（おき）ました
negative	（おき）ません	（おき）ませんでした

④ 毎朝 6時に 起きます。　　　I get up at six every morning.
⑤ あした 6時に 起きます。　　I'll get up at six tomorrow morning.
⑥ けさ 6時に 起きました。　　I got up at six this morning.

2) Question forms of verb sentences are made in the same way as those of noun sentences; i.e., the word order remains the same and か is added to the end of the sentence.

In answering such questions, the verbs in the questions are repeated. そうです or そうじゃ ありません (see Lesson 2) cannot be used.

⑦ きのう 勉強しましたか。　　　Did you study yesterday?
　…はい、勉強しました。　　　…Yes, I did.
　…いいえ、勉強しませんでした。…No, I didn't.

4

34

⑧ 毎朝 何時に 起きますか。 What time do you get up every morning?
…6時に 起きます。 …I get up at six.

4. | N (time)に V |

When a verb denotes a momentary action or movement, the time when it occurs is marked with the particle に. に is added when the noun before it uses a numeral. It can also be added to the days of the week, though it is not essential. When the noun does not use a numeral, に is not added.

⑨ 6時半に 起きます。 I get up at six thirty.
⑩ 7月2日に 日本へ 来ました。 I came to Japan on July 2nd. (L. 5)
⑪ 日曜日[に] 奈良へ 行きます。 I'm going to Nara on Sunday. (L. 5)
⑫ きのう 勉強しました。 I studied yesterday.

5. | N₁ から N₂ まで |

1) から indicates the starting time or place, and まで indicates the finishing time or place.

⑬ 9時から 5時まで 働きます。 I work from nine to five.
⑭ 大阪から 東京まで 3時間 かかります。

It takes three hours from Osaka to Tokyo. (L.11)

2) から and まで are not always used together.

⑮ 9時から 働きます。 I work from nine.

3) ～から, ～まで or ～から～まで is sometimes used with です added directly after either.

⑯ 銀行は 9時から 3時までです。 The bank is open from nine to three.
⑰ 昼休みは 12時からです。 Lunchtime starts at twelve.

6. | N₁ と N₂ |

The particle と connects two nouns in coordinate relation.

⑱ 銀行の 休みは 土曜日と 日曜日です。

The bank is closed on Saturdays and Sundays.

7. | S ね |

ね is attached to the end of a sentence to add feeling to what the speaker says. It shows the speaker's sympathy or the speaker's expectation that the listener will agree. In the latter usage, it is often used to confirm something.

⑲ 毎日 10時ごろまで 勉強します。 I study till about ten every day.
…大変ですね。 …That must be hard.
⑳ 山田さんの 電話番号は 871の 6813です。
…871の 6813ですね。
Mr. Yamada's telephone number is 871-6813.
…871-6813, right?

Lesson 5

I.   Vocabulary

いきます	行きます	go
きます	来ます	come
かえります	帰ります	go home, return
がっこう	学校	school
スーパー		supermarket
えき	駅	station
ひこうき	飛行機	airplane
ふね	船	ship
でんしゃ	電車	electric train
ちかてつ	地下鉄	subway, underground
しんかんせん	新幹線	the Shinkansen, the bullet train
バス		bus
タクシー		taxi
じてんしゃ	自転車	bicycle
あるいて	歩いて	on foot
ひと	人	person, people
ともだち	友達	friend
かれ	彼	he, boyfriend, lover
かのじょ	彼女	she, girlfriend, lover
かぞく	家族	family
ひとりで	一人で	alone, by oneself
せんしゅう	先週	last week
こんしゅう	今週	this week
らいしゅう	来週	next week
せんげつ	先月	last month
こんげつ	今月	this month
らいげつ	来月	next month
きょねん	去年	last year
ことし		this year
らいねん	来年	next year

－がつ	－月	-th month of the year
なんがつ	何月	what month
ついたち	1日	first day of the month
ふつか	2日	second, two days
みっか	3日	third, three days
よっか	4日	fourth, four days
いつか	5日	fifth, five days
むいか	6日	sixth, six days
なのか	7日	seventh, seven days
ようか	8日	eighth, eight days
ここのか	9日	ninth, nine days
とおか	10日	tenth, ten days
じゅうよっか	14日	fourteenth, fourteen days
はつか	20日	twentieth, twenty days
にじゅうよっか	24日	twenty fourth, twenty four days
－にち	－日	-th day of the month, － days
なんにち	何日	which day of the month, how many days
いつ		when
たんじょうび	誕生日	birthday
ふつう	普通	local (train)
きゅうこう	急行	rapid
とっきゅう	特急	express
つぎの	次の	next

◁会話▷

どう いたしまして。	You're welcome./Don't mention it.
－番線 <small>ばんせん</small>	platform －, -th platform

〜〜〜〜〜〜〜〜〜〜〜〜〜〜〜〜〜〜〜〜〜〜〜

博多 <small>はかた</small>	name of a town in Kyushu
伏見 <small>ふしみ</small>	name of a town in Kyoto
甲子園 <small>こうしえん</small>	name of a town near Osaka
大阪城 <small>おおさかじょう</small>	Osaka Castle, a famous castle in Osaka

II. Translation

Sentence Patterns

1. I [will] go to Kyoto.
2. I [will] go home by taxi.
3. I came to Japan with my family.

Example Sentences

1. Where will you go tomorrow?
   ···I will go to Nara.

2. Where did you go last Sunday?
   ···I didn't go anywhere.

3. How will you go to Tokyo?
   ···I will go by Shinkansen.

4. Who will you go to Tokyo with?
   ···I will go with Mr. Yamada.

5. When did you come to Japan?
   ···I came here on March 25th.

6. When is your birthday?
   ···It is June 13th.

Conversation

Does this train go to Koshien?

Santos:	Excuse me. How much is it to Koshien?
Woman :	It's 350 yen.
Santos:	350 yen? Thank you very much.
Woman :	You're welcome.

Santos:	Excuse me. What platform is it for Koshien?
Station employee:	No. 5.
Santos:	Thanks.

Santos:	Excuse me. Does this train go to Koshien?
Man:	No, it doesn't. The next "local train" does.
Santos:	Thank you very much.

III. Reference Words & Information

祝祭日（しゅくさいじつ）　NATIONAL HOLIDAYS

日付	名称	英語名
1月1日（がつついたち）	元日（がんじつ）	New Year's Day
1月第2月曜日（がつだいげつようび）**	成人の日（せいじんのひ）	Coming-of-Age Day
2月11日（がつにち）	建国記念の日（けんこくきねんのひ）	National Foundation Day
3月20日（がつはつか）*	春分の日（しゅんぶんのひ）	Vernal Equinox Day
4月29日（がつにち）	みどりの日（ひ）	Greenery Day
5月3日（がつみっか）	憲法記念日（けんぽうきねんび）	Constitution Memorial Day
5月4日（がつよっか）	国民の休日（こくみんのきゅうじつ）	Nation's Day
5月5日（がついつか）	こどもの日（ひ）	Children's Day
7月第3月曜日（がつだいげつようび）***	海の日（うみのひ）	Marine Day
9月第3月曜日（がつだいげつようび）***	敬老の日（けいろうのひ）	Respect-for-the-Aged Day
9月23日（がつにち）*	秋分の日（しゅうぶんのひ）	Autumnal Equinox Day
10月第2月曜日（がつだいげつようび）**	体育の日（たいいくのひ）	Health and Sports Day
11月3日（がつにち）	文化の日（ぶんかのひ）	Culture Day
11月23日（がつにち）	勤労感謝の日（きんろうかんしゃのひ）	Labor Thanksgiving Day
12月23日（がつにち）	天皇誕生日（てんのうたんじょうび）	The Emperor's Birthday

* Varies from year to year.

** The second Monday

*** The third Monday

 If a national holiday falls on a Sunday, the following Monday is taken off instead. From April 29th to May 5th is a series of holidays, called ゴールデンウィーク (Golden Week). Some big companies give a whole week's holiday to employees.

IV. Grammar Explanation

1. | N (place) へ 行きます／来ます／帰ります |

When a verb indicates movement to a certain place, the particle へ is put after
the place noun to show the direction of the move.

① 京都へ 行きます。   I will go to Kyoto.
② 日本へ 来ました。   I came to Japan.
③ うちへ 帰ります。   I will go home.

[Note] The particle へ is read え.

2. | どこ [へ] も 行きません／行きませんでした |

When an interrogative takes the particle も and the verb following it is
negative, all that is represented by the interrogative is denied.

④ どこ [へ] も 行きません。   I don't go anywhere.
⑤ 何も 食べません。   I don't eat anything. (L. 6)
⑥ だれも いません。   Nobody is there. (L. 10)

3. | N (vehicle)で 行きます／来ます／帰ります |

The particle で indicates a means or a method. When verbs denoting movement
(いきます, きます, かえります, etc.) are used with で, で indicates a
means of transportation. The noun preceding で is a vehicle in this
case.

⑦ 電車で 行きます。   I'll go by train.
⑧ タクシーで 来ました。   I came by taxi.

When you walk somewhere, you use the expression あるいて. In this case,
で is not used.

⑨ 駅から 歩いて 帰りました。   I walked home from the station.

4. | N (person/animal) と V |

When you do something with a person (or an animal), the person (or the
animal) is marked with the particle と.

⑩ 家族と 日本へ 来ました。   I came to Japan with my family.

If you do something alone, the expression ひとりで is used. In this case, と is
not used.

⑪ 一人で 東京へ 行きます。   I'll go to Tokyo alone.

5. いつ

To ask about time, the interrogatives using なん such as なんじ, なんようび and なんがつなんにち are used. Other than these, the interrogative いつ (when) is also used to ask when something will happen/happened. いつ does not take the particle に.

⑫ いつ 日本へ 来ましたか。   When did you come to Japan?
…3月25日に 来ました。   …I came on March 25th.

⑬ いつ 広島へ 行きますか。   When will you go to Hiroshima?
…来週 行きます。   …I'll go there next week.

6. S よ

よ is placed at the end of a sentence. It is used to emphasize information which the listener does not know, or to show that you are giving your judgement or views assertively.

⑭ この 電車は 甲子園へ 行きますか。
…いいえ、行きません。次の 普通ですよ。

Does this train go to Koshien?
…No, it doesn't. The next local train does.

⑮ 無理な ダイエットは 体に よくないですよ。

Excessive dieting is bad for your health. (L. 19)

41

Lesson 6

I.　Vocabulary

たべます	食べます	eat
のみます	飲みます	drink
すいます 　[たばこを 〜]	吸います	smoke [a cigarette]
みます	見ます	see, look at, watch
ききます	聞きます	hear, listen
よみます	読みます	read
かきます	書きます	write, draw, paint
かいます	買います	buy
とります 　[しゃしんを 〜]	撮ります 　[写真を 〜]	take [a photograph]
します		do
あいます 　[ともだちに 〜]	会います 　[友達に 〜]	meet [a friend]
ごはん		a meal, cooked rice
あさごはん	朝ごはん	breakfast
ひるごはん	昼ごはん	lunch
ばんごはん	晩ごはん	supper
パン		bread
たまご	卵	egg
にく	肉	meat
さかな	魚	fish
やさい	野菜	vegetable
くだもの	果物	fruit
みず	水	water
おちゃ	お茶	tea, green tea
こうちゃ	紅茶	black tea
ぎゅうにゅう 　（ミルク）	牛乳	milk
ジュース		juice
ビール		beer
[お]さけ	[お]酒	alcohol, Japanese rice wine

ビデオ		video tape, video deck
えいが	映画	movie
ＣＤ		CD, compact disc
てがみ	手紙	letter
レポート		report
しゃしん	写真	photograph
みせ	店	store, shop
レストラン		restaurant
にわ	庭	garden
しゅくだい	宿題	homework (〜を します: do homework)
テニス		tennis (〜を します: play tennis)
サッカー		soccer, football
		(〜を します: play soccer)
［お］はなみ	［お］花見	cherry-blossom viewing
		(〜を します: go cherry-blossom viewing)
なに	何	what
いっしょに		together
ちょっと		a little while, a little bit
いつも		always, usually
ときどき	時々	sometimes
それから		after that, and then
ええ		yes
いいですね。		That's good.
わかりました。		I see.

◁会話▷

何ですか。	Yes?
じゃ、また ［あした］。	See you [tomorrow].

〜〜〜〜〜〜〜〜〜〜〜〜〜〜〜

メキシコ	Mexico
大阪城公園	Osaka Castle park

6

43

II. Translation

Sentence Patterns

1. I drink juice.
2. I buy a newspaper at the station.
3. Won't you come to Kobe with me?
4. Let's take a rest for a little bit.

Example Sentences

1. Do you smoke?
   ···No, I don't.

2. What do you eat every morning?
   ···I have egg and toast.

3. What did you eat this morning?
   ···I didn't eat anything.

4. What did you do last Saturday?
   ···I studied Japanese. Then I saw a movie.
   On Sunday what did you do?
   ···I went to Nara with a friend.

5. Where did you buy that bag?
   ···I bought it in Mexico.

6. Won't you drink some beer with me?
   ···Yes, let's have a drink.

Conversation

Won't you join us?

Sato:	Mr. Miller.
Miller:	Yes?
Sato:	I'm going to enjoy cherry-blossom viewing with my friends tomorrow.
	Won't you join us, Mr. Miller?
Miller:	That sounds nice. Where will you go?
Sato:	Osakajo-Koen.
Miller:	What time?
Sato:	At ten o'clock. Let's meet at Osakajo-Koen Station.
Miller:	OK.
Sato:	Well, see you tomorrow.

III. Reference Words & Information

食べ物　FOOD

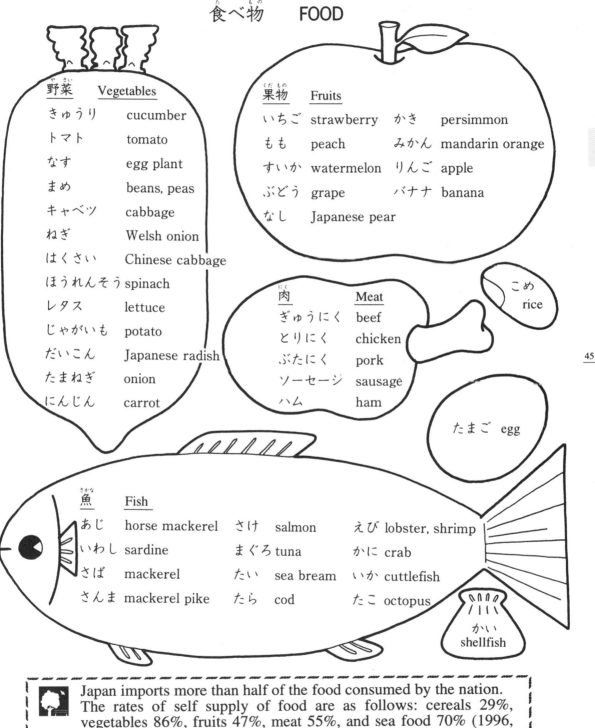

野菜　Vegetables

きゅうり	cucumber
トマト	tomato
なす	egg plant
まめ	beans, peas
キャベツ	cabbage
ねぎ	Welsh onion
はくさい	Chinese cabbage
ほうれんそう	spinach
レタス	lettuce
じゃがいも	potato
だいこん	Japanese radish
たまねぎ	onion
にんじん	carrot

果物　Fruits

いちご	strawberry	かき	persimmon
もも	peach	みかん	mandarin orange
すいか	watermelon	りんご	apple
ぶどう	grape	バナナ	banana
なし	Japanese pear		

肉　Meat

ぎゅうにく	beef
とりにく	chicken
ぶたにく	pork
ソーセージ	sausage
ハム	ham

こめ　rice

たまご　egg

魚　Fish

あじ	horse mackerel	さけ	salmon	えび	lobster, shrimp
いわし	sardine	まぐろ	tuna	かに	crab
さば	mackerel	たい	sea bream	いか	cuttlefish
さんま	mackerel pike	たら	cod	たこ	octopus

かい　shellfish

6

45

IV. Grammar Explanation

1. ┃ N を V (transitive) ┃

を is used to indicate the direct object of a transitive verb.

① ジュースを 飲みます。   I drink juice.

[Note] を and お are pronounced the same. The former is used only in writing the particle.

2. ┃ N を します ┃

The words used as the objects of the verb します cover a fairly wide range. します means that the action denoted by the noun is performed. Some examples are shown below.

1) to "play" sports or games
   サッカーを します   play football
   トランプを します   play cards

2) to "hold" gatherings
   パーティーを します   give a party
   会議を します   hold a meeting

3) to "do" something
   宿題を します   do homework
   仕事を します   do one's work

3. 何を しますか

This is a question to ask what someone does.

② 月曜日 何を しますか。   What will you do on Monday?
 …京都へ 行きます。   …I'll go to Kyoto.
③ きのう 何を しましたか。   What did you do yesterday?
 …サッカーを しました。   …I played football.

[Note] You can make a word expressing time the topic by adding は.

④ 月曜日は 何を しますか。   On Monday what will you do?
 …京都へ 行きます。   …I'll go to Kyoto.

4. なん and なに

Both なん and なに mean "what."

1) なん is used in the following cases.

 (1) When it precedes a word whose first mora is either in the た, だ or な-row.

 ⑤ それは 何ですか。   What is that?
 ⑥ 何の 本ですか。   What is the book about?
 ⑦ 寝る まえに、何と 言いますか。
   What do you say before going to bed? (L. 21)

(2) When it is followed by a counter suffix or the like.

⑧ テレサちゃんは 何歳ですか。　　How old is Teresa?

2) なに is used in all other cases.

⑨ 何を 買いますか。　　　　　What will you buy?

5. N (place) で V

When added after a noun denoting a place, で indicates the place where an action occurs.

⑩ 駅で 新聞を 買います。　　　I buy the newspaper at the station.

6. V ませんか

When you want to invite someone to do something, this expression is used.

⑪ いっしょに 京都へ 行きませんか。
　…ええ、いいですね。

Won't you come to Kyoto with us?
　…That's a nice idea.

7. V ましょう

This expression is used when a speaker is positively inviting the listener to do something with the speaker. It is also used when responding positively to an invitation.

⑫ ちょっと 休みましょう。　　　Let's have a break.

⑬ いっしょに 昼ごはんを 食べませんか。
　…ええ、食べましょう。

Won't you have lunch with me?
　…Yes, let's go and eat.

[Note] An invitation using V ませんか shows more consideration to the listener's will than that using V ましょう.

8. お〜

You learned in Lesson 3 that the prefix お is attached to words regarding the listener or the person being referred to to show respect (e.g.,[お]くに country).

　お is also attached to various other words when the speaker is speaking politely (e.g.,[お]さけ alcohol,[お]はなみ cherry-blossom viewing).

　There are some words that are usually used with お without meaning respect or politeness (e.g., おちゃ tea, おかね money).

Lesson 7

I. Vocabulary

きります	切ります	cut, slice
おくります	送ります	send
あげます		give
もらいます		receive
かします	貸します	lend
かります	借ります	borrow
おしえます	教えます	teach
ならいます	習います	learn
かけます		make [a telephone call]
[でんわを ～]	［電話を ～］	
て	手	hand, arm
はし		chopsticks
スプーン		spoon
ナイフ		knife
フォーク		fork
はさみ		scissors
ファクス		fax
ワープロ		word processor
パソコン		personal computer
パンチ		punch
ホッチキス		stapler
セロテープ		Scotch tape, clear adhesive tape
けしゴム	消しゴム	eraser
かみ	紙	paper
はな	花	flower, blossom
シャツ		shirt
プレゼント		present, gift
にもつ	荷物	baggage, parcel
おかね	お金	money
きっぷ	切符	ticket
クリスマス		Christmas

ちち	父	(my) father
はは	母	(my) mother
おとうさん	お父さん	(someone else's) father
おかあさん	お母さん	(someone else's) mother

もう	already
まだ	not yet
これから	from now on, soon

[〜、]すてきですね。	What a nice [〜]!

◀会話▶

ごめんください。	Excuse me./Anybody home?/May I come in? (an expression used by a visitor)
いらっしゃい。	How nice of you to come. (lit. Welcome.)
どうぞ お上がり ください。	Do come in.
失礼します。	Thank you./May I? (lit. I'm afraid I'll be disturbing you.)
[〜は] いかがですか。	Won't you have [〜]?/Would you like to have [〜]? (used when offering something)
いただきます。	Thank you./I accept. (said before starting to eat or drink)
旅行	trip, tour (〜を します: travel, make a trip)
お土産	souvenir, present

~~~~~~~~~~~~~~~~~~~~~~~~~~~~~~~~~~~~~~

ヨーロッパ	Europe
スペイン	Spain

49

II. Translation

Sentence Patterns

1. I write letters with a word processor.
2. I [will] give some flowers to Ms. Kimura.
3. I received some chocolates from Ms. Karina.

Example Sentences

1. Did you study Japanese through television?
   ···No, I studied it through radio.
2. Do you write reports in Japanese?
   ···No. I write them in English.
3. What is "Good-bye" in Japanese?
   ···It is "Sayonara."
4. Who will you write Christmas cards to?
   ···To my family and friends.
5. What is that?
   ···It's a pocket notebook. I received it from Mr. Yamada.
6. Have you bought your Shinkansen ticket?
   ···Yes, I have.
7. Have you finished lunch?
   ···No, not yet. I am going to eat now.

Conversation

Hello

Jose Santos:	Hello.
Yamada Ichiro:	Hello. Please come in.
Jose Santos:	Thank you.

Yamada Tomoko:	How about a cup of coffee?
Maria Santos:	Thank you.

Yamada Tomoko:	Here you are.
Maria Santos:	Thank you.
	This spoon is nice, isn't it?
Yamada Tomoko:	Yes, it is. Someone in my company gave it to me.
	It's a souvenir of her trip to Europe.

III. Reference Words & Information

家族　FAMILY

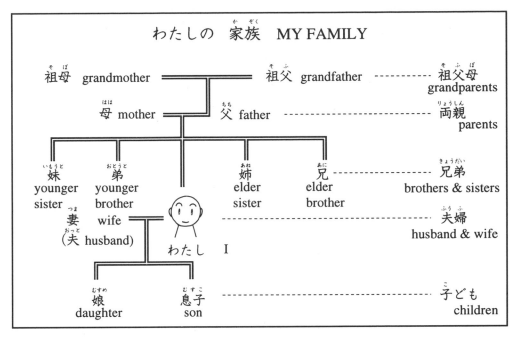

わたしの　家族　MY FAMILY

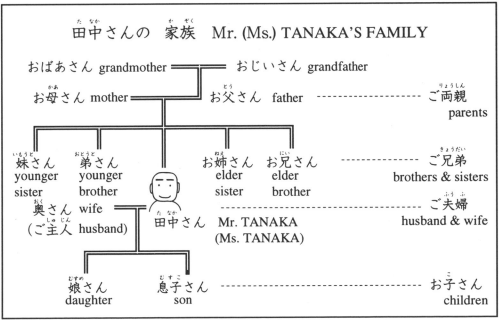

田中さんの　家族　Mr. (Ms.) TANAKA'S FAMILY

IV. Grammar Explanation

1. | N (tool/means)で　V |

The particle で indicates a method or a mean used for an action.

① はしで　食べます。　　　　　　　　I eat with chopsticks.
② 日本語で　レポートを　書きます。　I write a report in Japanese.

2. "Word/Sentence" は　〜語で　何ですか

This question is used to ask how to say a word or a sentence in other languages.

③ 「ありがとう」は　英語で　何ですか。
　 … 「Thank you」です。
　 What's "ありがとう" in English?
　 … It's "Thank you."
④ 「Thank you」は　日本語で　何ですか。
　 … 「ありがとう」です。
　 What's "Thank you" in Japanese?
　 … It's " ありがとう."

3. | N (person) に　あげます, etc. |

Verbs like あげます, かします, おしえます, etc., need persons to whom you give, lend, teach, etc. The persons are marked with に.

⑤ 山田さんは　木村さんに　花を　あげました。
　 Mr. Yamada gave flowers to Ms. Kimura.
⑥ イーさんに　本を　貸しました。
　 I lent my book to Ms. Lee.
⑦ 太郎君に　英語を　教えます。
　 I teach Taro English.

[Note] With verbs like おくります, でんわを　かけます, etc., place nouns can be used instead of N(person). In this case, the particle へ is sometimes used instead of に.

⑧ 会社に　電話を　かけます。
　 （へ）
　 I'll call my office.

4. N (person) に もらいます, etc.

Verbs like もらいます, かります and ならいます express actions from the receiving side. The persons from whom you receive those actions are marked with に.

⑨ 木村さんは 山田さんに 花を もらいました。

　　Ms. Kimura received flowers from Mr. Yamada.

⑩ カリナさんに ＣＤを 借りました。

　　I borrowed a CD from Ms. Karina.

⑪ ワンさんに 中国語を 習います。

　　I learn Chinese from Mr. Wang.

から is sometimes used instead of に in this sentence pattern. When you receive something from an organization like a school or a company, only から is used.

⑫ 木村さんは 山田さんから 花を もらいました。

　　Ms. Kimura received flowers from Mr. Yamada.

⑬ 銀行から お金を 借りました。

　　I borrowed some money from the bank.

5. もう Ｖました

もう means "already" and is used with Ｖました. In this case, Ｖました means that the action has been finished.

　The answer to the question もう Ｖましたか is はい、もう Ｖました or いいえ、まだです.

⑭ もう 荷物を 送りましたか。　　　Have you sent the parcel yet?

　…はい、[もう] 送りました。　　　…Yes, I have [already sent it].

　…いいえ、まだです。　　　　　　…No, not yet.

In giving a negative answer to this type of question, you should not use Ｖませんでした, as this simply means you did not do the specified task rather than you have not done it yet.

7

Lesson 8

I. Vocabulary

ハンサム[な]		handsome
きれい[な]		beautiful, clean
しずか[な]	静か[な]	quiet
にぎやか[な]		lively
ゆうめい[な]	有名[な]	famous
しんせつ[な]	親切[な]	kind
げんき[な]	元気[な]	healthy, sound, cheerful
ひま[な]	暇[な]	free (time)
べんり[な]	便利[な]	convenient
すてき[な]		fine, nice, wonderful
おおきい	大きい	big, large
ちいさい	小さい	small, little
あたらしい	新しい	new
ふるい	古い	old (not of age)
いい（よい）		good
わるい	悪い	bad
あつい	暑い、熱い	hot
さむい	寒い	cold (referring to temperature)
つめたい	冷たい	cold (referring to touch)
むずかしい	難しい	difficult
やさしい	易しい	easy
たかい	高い	expensive, tall, high
やすい	安い	inexpensive
ひくい	低い	low
おもしろい		interesting
おいしい		delicious, tasty
いそがしい	忙しい	busy
たのしい	楽しい	enjoyable
しろい	白い	white
くろい	黒い	black
あかい	赤い	red
あおい	青い	blue
さくら	桜	cherry (blossom)
やま	山	mountain

まち	町	town, city
たべもの	食べ物	food
くるま	車	car, vehicle
ところ	所	place
りょう	寮	dormitory
べんきょう	勉強	study
せいかつ	生活	life
［お］しごと	［お］仕事	work, business
		(～を します: do one's job, work)

どう		how
どんな ～		what kind of ～
どれ		which one (of three or more)
とても		very
あまり		not so (used with negatives)
そして		and (used to connect sentences)
～が、～		～, but ～

おげんきですか。　お元気ですか。	How are you?
そうですね。	Well let me see. (pausing)

◁会話▷

日本の 生活に 慣れましたか。	Have you got used to the life in Japan?
［～、］もう 一杯 いかがですか。	Won't you have another cup of ［～］?
いいえ、けっこうです。	No, thank you.
もう ～です［ね］。	It's already ～[, isn't it?].
そろそろ 失礼します。	It's almost time to leave now.
また いらっしゃって ください。	Please come again.

~~~~~~~~~~~~~~~~~~~~~~~~~~~~~~~~~~

富士山	Mt. Fuji, the highest mountain in Japan
琵琶湖	Lake Biwa, the biggest lake in Japan
シャンハイ	Shanghai (上海)
「七人の 侍」	"The Seven Samurai," a classic movie by Akira Kurosawa
金閣寺	Kinkakuji Temple (the Golden Pavilion)

II. Translation

Sentence Patterns

1. Cherry blossoms are beautiful.
2. Mt. Fuji is high.
3. Cherry blossoms are beautiful flowers.
4. Mt. Fuji is a high mountain.

Example Sentences

1. Is Osaka lively?
   ···Yes, it is.

2. Is the water of Lake Biwa clean?
   ···No, it is not so clean.

3. Is it cold in Beijing now?
   ···Yes, it is very cold.
   Is it cold in Shanghai, too?
   ···No, it is not so cold.

4. Is that dictionary good?
   ···No, it is not so good.

5. How do you like the subway in Tokyo?
   ···It is clean. And it is convenient.

6. I saw a movie yesterday.
   ···What kind of movie was it?
   It was "The Seven Samurai." It is old, but a very interesting movie.

7. Which is Mr. Miller's umbrella?
   ···That blue one is.

Conversation

It's almost time to leave

Yamada Ichiro:	Have you got accustomed to living in Japan, Maria?
Maria Santos:	Yes, I have. I enjoy it every day.
Yamada Ichiro:	Really? Mr. Santos, how is your work?
Jose Santos:	Well, it's busy, but interesting.

Yamada Tomoko:	Would you like another cup of coffee?
Maria Santos:	No, thank you.

Jose Santos:	Oh, it's eight o'clock now. We must be going.
Yamada Ichiro:	You must?
Maria Santos:	Thank you for everything today.
Yamada Tomoko:	Our pleasure. Please come again.

III. Reference Words & Information

色・味　COLOR & TASTE
（いろ・あじ）

色 Color
（いろ）

noun	adjective	noun	adjective
白 white（しろ）	白い（しろ）	黄色 yellow（き いろ）	黄色い（き いろ）
黒 black（くろ）	黒い（くろ）	茶色 brown（ちゃ いろ）	茶色い（ちゃ いろ）
赤 red（あか）	赤い（あか）	ピンク pink	—
青 blue（あお）	青い（あお）	オレンジ orange	—
緑 green（みどり）	—	グレー gray	—
紫 purple（むらさき）	—	ベージュ beige	—

味 Taste
（あじ）

甘い sweet（あま）　　辛い hot（から）　　苦い bitter（にが）　　塩辛い salty（しお から）

酸っぱい sour（す）　　濃い thick, strong（こ）　　薄い thin, weak（うす）

  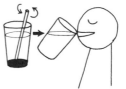

 春・夏・秋・冬 Spring·Summer·Autumn·Winter
（はる・なつ・あき・ふゆ）

There are four seasons in Japan, spring (March, April, May), summer (June, July, August), autumn (September, October, November), and winter (December, January, February). The average temperature varies from place to place, but the change patterns are almost the same (see the graph).

The hottest month is August and the coldest, January or February. So Japanese people feel that "summer is hot," "autumn is cool," "winter is cold," and "spring is warm."

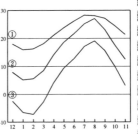

① NAHA (OKINAWA)
② TOKYO
③ ABASHIRI (HOKKAIDO)

IV. Grammar Explanation

1. Adjectives

Adjectives are used as 1) predicates and 2) noun modifiers. They inflect and are divided into two groups, い-adjectives and な-adjectives, according to the inflection.

2.
> N は　な-adj [な] です
> N は　い-adj (〜い) です

1) です at the end of an adjective sentence shows the speaker's polite attitude toward the listener. An い-adjective with い at the end comes before です, whereas a な-adjective without [な] comes before です.

① ワット先生は　親切です。　　　　　Mr. Watt is kind.
② 富士山は　高いです。　　　　　　Mt. Fuji is high.

です is used when a sentence is non-past and affirmative.

2) な-adj [な] じゃ ありません
The negative form of な-adj [な] です is な-adj [な] じゃ ありません.
(な-adj [な] では ありません)

③ あそこは　静かじゃ ありません。　It's not quiet there.
　　　　　　　（では）

3) い-adj (〜い) です → 〜くないです
To make the negative form of an い- adjective, い at the end of the い-adjective is altered to くない.

④ この 本は　おもしろくないです。　This book is not interesting.

The negative for いいです is よくないです.

4) Questions using adjective sentences are made in the same way as those using noun or verb sentences. In answering a question, you repeat the adjective used in the question. そうです or そうじゃ ありません cannot be used.

⑤ ペキンは　寒いですか。　　　　　Is it cold in Beijing?
　…はい、寒いです。　　　　　　…Yes, it is.
⑥ 琵琶湖の　水は　きれいですか。　Is the water of Lake Biwa clean?
　…いいえ、きれいじゃ ありません。…No, it isn't.

3.
> な-adj な　N
> い-adj (〜い) N

An adjective is put before a noun to modify it. A な-adjective needs な before a noun.

⑦ ワット先生は　親切な 先生です。　Mr. Watt is a kind teacher.
⑧ 富士山は　高い 山です。　　　　Mt. Fuji is a high mountain.

4. とても／あまり

とても and あまり are adverbs of degree. Both come before the adjectives they are modifying.

とても is used in affirmative sentences, and means "very." あまり is used in negative sentences. あまり and a negative form mean "not very."

⑨ ペキンは とても 寒いです。

Beijing is very cold.

⑩ これは とても 有名な 映画です。

This is a very famous movie.

⑪ シャンハイは あまり 寒くないです。

Shanghai is not very cold.

⑫ さくら大学は あまり 有名な 大学じゃ ありません。

Sakura University is not a very famous university.

5. Nは どうですか

This question is used to ask an impression or an opinion about a thing, place or person, etc., that the listener has experienced, visited or met.

⑬ 日本の 生活は どうですか。　　How is the life in Japan?

　…楽しいです。　　　　　　　　…It's enjoyable.

6. N₁は どんな N₂ですか

When the speaker wants the listener to describe or explain N_1, this question pattern is used. N_2 denotes the category N_1 belongs to. The interrogative どんな is always followed by a noun.

⑭ 奈良は どんな 町ですか。　　What kind of town is Nara?

　…古い 町です。　　　　　　　…It's an old town.

7. S₁が、S₂

が is a conjunctive particle, meaning "but." It is used to link sentences.

⑮ 日本の 食べ物は おいしいですが、高いです。

Japanese food is good, but expensive.

8. どれ

This interrogative is used to ask the listener to choose or designate one from more than two things concretely shown or named.

⑯ ミラーさんの 傘は どれですか。Which is Mr. Miller's umbrella?

　…あの 青い 傘です。　　　　　…That blue one is.

Lesson 9

I.   Vocabulary

わかります		understand
あります		have
すき[な]	好き[な]	like
きらい[な]	嫌い[な]	dislike
じょうず[な]	上手[な]	good at
へた[な]	下手[な]	poor at
りょうり	料理	dish (cooked food), cooking
のみもの	飲み物	drinks
スポーツ		sport (〜を します: play sports)
やきゅう	野球	baseball (〜を します: play baseball)
ダンス		dance (〜を します: dance)
おんがく	音楽	music
うた	歌	song
クラシック		classical music
ジャズ		jazz
コンサート		concert
カラオケ		karaoke
かぶき	歌舞伎	Kabuki (traditional Japanese musical drama)
え	絵	picture, drawing
じ	字	letter, character
かんじ	漢字	Chinese characters
ひらがな		Hiragana script
かたかな		Katakana script
ローマじ	ローマ字	the Roman alphabet
こまかい おかね	細かい お金	small change
チケット		ticket
じかん	時間	time
ようじ	用事	something to do, errand
やくそく	約束	appointment, promise

ごしゅじん	ご主人	(someone else's) husband
おっと／しゅじん	夫／主人	(my) husband
おくさん	奥さん	(someone else's) wife
つま／かない	妻／家内	(my) wife
こども	子ども	child

よく		well, much
だいたい		mostly, roughly
たくさん		many, much
すこし	少し	a little, a few
ぜんぜん	全然	not at all (used with negatives)
はやく	早く、速く	early, quickly, fast

〜から	because 〜
どうして	why

ざんねんです［ね］。残念です［ね］。	I'm sorry (to hear that)./That's a pity.
すみません。	I am sorry.

◁会話▷

もしもし	hello (used on the phone)
ああ	oh
いっしょに いかがですか。	Won't you join me (us)?
［〜は］ ちょっと……。	[〜] is a bit difficult. (an euphemism used when declining an invitation)
だめですか。	So you cannot (come)?
また 今度 お願いします。	Please ask me again some other time. (used when refusing an invitation indirectly, considering someone's feelings)

〜〜〜〜〜〜〜〜〜〜〜〜〜〜〜〜〜〜〜〜〜〜〜〜

小沢 征爾	famous Japanese conductor (1935－)

II. Translation

Sentence Patterns

1. I like Italian cuisine.
2. I understand Japanese a little.
3. Today is my child's birthday, so I will go home early.

Example Sentences

1. Do you like alcohol?
   ···No, I don't.

2. What kind of sports do you like?
   ···I like soccer.

3. Is Ms. Karina good at drawing pictures?
   ···Yes, she is very good at it.

4. Do you understand Indonesian, Mr. Tanaka?
   ···No, I do not understand it at all.

5. Do you have any small change?
   ···No, I don't.

6. Do you read newspapers every morning?
   ···No, as I don't have the time, I don't.

7. Why did you go home early yesterday?
   ···Because I had something to do.

Conversation

That's too bad

Miller:	Hello. This is Miller.
Kimura:	It's you, Mr. Miller. Good evening. How are you?
Miller:	Fine. Thank you.
	Well, Ms. Kimura. How would you like to go to a concert by Seiji Ozawa?
Kimura:	That sounds nice. When will it be?
Miller:	It's on Friday night of next week.
Kimura:	Friday?
	Friday's a bit difficult.
Miller:	So you can't come?
Kimura:	I have arranged to meet a friend on Friday night.
Miller:	You have. I'm sorry to hear that.
Kimura:	I am, too. Please invite me again some other time.

III. Reference Words & Information

音楽・スポーツ・映画　MUSIC, SPORTS & MOVIES

音楽 Music

ポップス	pop
ロック	rock
ジャズ	jazz
ラテン	Latin American music
クラシック	classical music
民謡	folk music
演歌	traditional Japanese popular songs
ミュージカル	musical
オペラ	opera

映画 Film

ＳＦ	SF film
ホラー	horror film
アニメ	animated film
ドキュメンタリー	documentary film
恋愛	romantic film
ミステリー	mystery film
文芸	movie based on a classic work
戦争	war film
アクション	action film
喜劇	comedy film

スポーツ Sports

ソフトボール	softball	野球	baseball
サッカー	soccer	卓球／ピンポン	ping-pong
ラグビー	rugby football	相撲	sumo
バレーボール	volleyball	柔道	judo
バスケットボール	basketball	剣道	Japanese fencing
テニス	tennis	水泳	swimming
ボーリング	bowling		
スキー	skiing		
スケート	skating		

IV. Grammar Explanation

1.
> **N** が あります／わかります
> **N** が 好きです／嫌いです／上手です／下手です

The object of a transitive verb is marked with を. However, objects of the verbs あります and わかります are marked with が.

Such adjectives as すきです, きらいです, じょうずです and へたです require objects, and these are marked with が, too. The verbs and adjectives whose objects are marked with が are those kinds that describe preference, ability, possession and the like.

① わたしは イタリア料理が 好きです。　I like Italian food.
② わたしは 日本語が わかります。　I understand Japanese.
③ わたしは 車が あります。　I have a car.

2. どんな N

Other than the usage you learned in Lesson 8, どんな is also used to ask the listener to name one from a group which the noun after どんな denotes.

④ どんな スポーツが 好きですか。　What sports do you like?
　…サッカーが 好きです。　…I like football.

3. よく／だいたい／たくさん／少し／あまり／全然

These adverbs are put before verbs when they modify them. The following is a summary of their usage.

degree	adverb + affirmative	adverb + negative
high ↑ ↓ low	よく　　　わかります だいたい　わかります すこし　　わかります	あまり　わかりません ぜんぜん わかりません

amount	adverb + affirmative	adverb + negative
large ↑ ↓ small	たくさん あります すこし　　あります	あまり　ありません ぜんぜん ありません

⑤ 英語が よく わかります。 I understand English very well.

⑥ 英語が 少し わかります。 I understand English a little.

⑦ 英語が あまり わかりません。 I don't understand English so well.

⑧ お金が たくさん あります。 I have a lot of money.

⑨ お金が 全然 ありません。 I don't have any money.

[Note] すこし and ぜんぜん can also modify adjectives.

⑩ ここは 少し 寒いです。 It's a little cold here.

⑪ あの 映画は 全然 おもしろくないです。

That movie is not interesting at all.

4. S₁ から、 S₂

から connects two sentences together to denote a causal relationship. S₁ is the reason for S₂.

⑫ 時間が ありませんから、新聞を 読みません。

Because I don't have time, I don't read the newspaper.

You can also state S₂ first and add the reason after it.

⑬ 毎朝 新聞を 読みますか。

…いいえ、読みません。時間が ありませんから。

Do you read a newspaper every morning?

…No, I don't. Because I have no time.

5. どうして

The interrogative どうして is used to ask a reason. The answer needs から at the end.

⑭ どうして 朝 新聞を 読みませんか。

…時間が ありませんから。

Why don't you read a newspaper in the morning?

…Because I don't have time.

The question どうしてですか is also used to ask the reason for what the other person has said.

⑮ きょうは 早く 帰ります。 I'll go home early today.

…どうしてですか。 …Why?

子どもの 誕生日ですから。 Because today's my child's birthday.

Lesson 10

I.   Vocabulary

います		exist, be (referring to animate things)
あります		exist, be (referring to inanimate things)
いろいろ[な]		various
おとこの ひと	男の 人	man
おんなの ひと	女の 人	woman
おとこの こ	男の 子	boy
おんなの こ	女の 子	girl
いぬ	犬	dog
ねこ	猫	cat
き	木	tree, wood
もの	物	thing
フィルム		film
でんち	電池	battery
はこ	箱	box
スイッチ		switch
れいぞうこ	冷蔵庫	refrigerator
テーブル		table
ベッド		bed
たな	棚	shelf
ドア		door
まど	窓	window
ポスト		mailbox, postbox
ビル		building
こうえん	公園	park
きっさてん	喫茶店	coffee shop
ほんや	本屋	bookstore
〜や	〜屋	〜 store
のりば	乗り場	a fixed place to catch taxis, trains, etc.
けん	県	prefecture

うえ	上	on, above, over
した	下	under, below, beneath
まえ	前	front, before
うしろ		back, behind
みぎ	右	right [side]
ひだり	左	left [side]
なか	中	in, inside
そと	外	outside
となり	隣	next, next door
ちかく	近く	near, vicinity
あいだ	間	between, among

〜や 〜[など]		〜, 〜, and so on
いちばん 〜		the most 〜 (いちばん うえ: the top)
−だんめ	−段目	the -th shelf (だん is the counter for shelves)

◁会話▷

［どうも］すみません。	Thank you.
チリソース	chili sauce
奥	the back
スパイス・コーナー	spice corner

〜〜〜〜〜〜〜〜〜〜〜〜〜〜〜〜〜〜〜〜〜

東京ディズニーランド	Tokyo Disneyland
ユニューヤ・ストア	fictitious supermarket

II. Translation

Sentence Patterns

1. Ms. Sato is over there.
2. There is a photo on the desk.
3. My family is in New York.
4. Tokyo Disneyland is in Chiba Prefecture.

Example Sentences

1. You see that man over there. Who is that?
   ···He is Mr. Matsumoto of IMC.

2. Is there a telephone near here?
   ···Yes, it is over there.

3. Who is in the garden?
   ···Nobody is. There is a cat.

4. What is there in the box?
   ···There are old letters and photos and so on.

5. Where is Mr. Miller?
   ···He is in the meeting room.

6. Where is the post office?
   ···It is near the station. It is in front of the bank.

Conversation

Do you have chili sauce in this store?

Miller:	Excuse me. Where is Yunyu-ya Store?
Woman:	Yunyu-ya Store?
	You see that white building over there?
	The store is in that building.
Miller:	I see. Thank you.
Woman:	Not at all.

Miller:	Excuse me, do you have chili sauce?
Shop assistant:	Yes.
	There is a spice corner on the right-hand side at the back.
	Chili sauce is on the second rack from the bottom.
Miller:	I see. Thanks.

III. Reference Words & Information

うちの中 INSIDE THE HOUSE

① 玄関　entrance hall
② トイレ　toilet
③ 風呂場　bathroom
④ 洗面所　washroom
⑤ 台所　kitchen
⑥ 食堂　dining room
⑦ 居間　living room
⑧ 寝室　bedroom
⑨ 廊下　hallway
⑩ ベランダ　balcony

How to Use a Japanese Bath

① Wash and rinse yourself in the tiled area before getting in the bath.

② Soap and shampoo should never be used in the bath. The bath is for soaking and relaxing.

③ When you get out of the bath, you don't drain the water as someone else may wish to use it. Put a cover on the bath.

How to Use the Toilet

Japanese style

Western style

IV. Grammar Explanation

1. $\boxed{\text{N が あります/います}}$

This sentence pattern is used to indicate the existence or presence of a thing(s) or person(s). The thing(s) or person(s) in such a sentence is treated as the subject and marked with the particle が.

1) あります is used when what is present is inanimate or does not move by itself. Things, plants and places belong in this category.

　① コンピューターが あります。　　There is a computer.
　② 桜が あります。　　　　　　　　There are cherry trees.
　③ 公園が あります。　　　　　　　There is a park.

2) When what is present is animate and moves by itself, います is used. People and animals belong in this category.

　④ 男の 人が います。　　　　　　There is a man.
　⑤ 犬が います。　　　　　　　　　There is a dog.

2. $\boxed{\text{N}_1 \text{(place) に N}_2 \text{が あります/います}}$

1) The place where N₂ is present is indicated by the particle に.

　⑥ わたしの 部屋に 机が あります。　　There is a desk in my room.
　⑦ 事務所に ミラーさんが います。　　Mr. Miller is in the office.

2) You can ask what or who is present at/in the place by using this pattern. The interrogative なに is used for things and だれ is used for persons.

　⑧ 地下に 何が ありますか。　　　What is there in the basement?
　　…レストランが あります。　　　…There are restaurants.
　⑨ 受付に だれが いますか。　　　Who is at the reception desk?
　　…木村さんが います。　　　　　…Ms. Kimura is there.

3. $\boxed{\text{N}_1 \text{は N}_2 \text{(place) に あります/います}}$

1) In this sentence pattern, the speaker picks up N₁ as the topic, and explains where it is. The topic should be something or someone that both the speaker and the listener know about. The particle attached to N₁ is not が, which marks the subject, but は, which marks the topic.

　⑩ 東京ディズニーランドは 千葉県に あります。

　　Tokyo Disneyland is in Chiba Prefecture.

　⑪ ミラーさんは 事務所に います。　　Mr. Miller is in the office.

2) When you ask where N₁ is, this sentence pattern is used.

　⑫ 東京ディズニーランドは どこに ありますか。
　　…千葉県に あります。
　　Where is Tokyo Disneyland?
　　…It's in Chiba Prefecture.
　⑬ ミラーさんは どこに いますか。　　Where is Mr. Miller?
　　…事務所に います。　　　　　　　…He's in the office.

[Note] です is sometimes used to replace a verb predicate when the predicate is obvious. The sentence N₁ は N₂(place)に あります／います can be replaced by the sentence N₁ は N₂(place)です, which you learned in Lesson 3.

⑭ 東京ディズニーランドは どこに ありますか。
…千葉県です。
Where is Tokyo Disneyland?
…It's in Chiba Prefecture.

4. | N₁(thing/person/place) の N₂(position) |

うえ, した, まえ, うしろ, みぎ, ひだり, なか, そと, となり, ちかく and あいだ are nouns denoting position.

⑮ 机の 上に 写真が あります。　There is a picture on the desk.
⑯ 郵便局は 銀行の 隣に あります。　The post office is next to the bank.

[Note] As these are place nouns, not only に but also particles like で can come after them.

⑰ 駅の 近くで 友達に 会いました。　I met a friend near the station.

5. | N₁ や N₂ |

Nouns are connected in coordinate relation by the particle や. While と enumerates all the items, や shows a few representative items. Sometimes など is put after the last noun to explicitly express that there are also some other things of the kind.

⑱ 箱の 中に 手紙や 写真が あります。
There are letters, pictures and so on in the box.

⑲ 箱の 中に 手紙や 写真などが あります。
There are letters, pictures and so on in the box.

6. Word (s) ですか

The particle か has the function to confirm. The speaker picks up a word or words he/she wants to confirm and confirms it (them) using this pattern.

⑳ すみません。ユニューヤ・ストアは どこですか。
…ユニューヤ・ストアですか。あの ビルの 中です。
Excuse me, but where is Yunyu-ya Store?
…Yunyu-ya Store? It's in that building.

7. チリソースは ありませんか

The expression チリソースは ありませんか is found in the conversation of this lesson. By using the negative form ありませんか instead of ありますか, you can be indirect and polite, showing that you are prepared for a negative answer.

Lesson 11

I. Vocabulary

います [こどもが 〜]	[子どもが 〜]	have [a child]
います [にほんに 〜]	[日本に 〜]	stay, be [in Japan]
かかります		take (referring to time or money)
やすみます [かいしゃを 〜]	休みます [会社を 〜]	take a day off [work]
ひとつ	1つ	one (used when counting things)
ふたつ	2つ	two
みっつ	3つ	three
よっつ	4つ	four
いつつ	5つ	five
むっつ	6つ	six
ななつ	7つ	seven
やっつ	8つ	eight
ここのつ	9つ	nine
とお	10	ten
いくつ		how many
ひとり	1人	one person
ふたり	2人	two persons
〜にん	〜人	〜 people
〜だい	〜台	(counter for machines, cars, etc.)
〜まい	〜枚	(counter for paper, stamps, etc.)
〜かい	〜回	〜 times
りんご		apple
みかん		mandarin orange
サンドイッチ		sandwich
カレー[ライス]		curry [and rice]
アイスクリーム		ice cream
きって	切手	postage stamp
はがき		post card
ふうとう	封筒	envelope
そくたつ	速達	special delivery
かきとめ	書留	registered mail

11

72

エアメール		airmail
（こうくうびん）	（航空便）	
ふなびん	船便	sea mail
りょうしん	両親	parents
きょうだい	兄弟	brothers and sisters
あに	兄	(my) elder brother
おにいさん	お兄さん	(someone else's) elder brother
あね	姉	(my) elder sister
おねえさん	お姉さん	(someone else's) elder sister
おとうと	弟	(my) younger brother
おとうとさん	弟さん	(someone else's) younger brother
いもうと	妹	(my) younger sister
いもうとさん	妹さん	(someone else's) younger sister
がいこく	外国	foreign country
－じかん	－時間	－ hours
－しゅうかん	－週間	－ weeks
－かげつ	－か月	－ months
－ねん	－年	－ years
～ぐらい		about ～
どのくらい		how long
ぜんぶで	全部で	in total
みんな		all, everything
～だけ		only ～
いらっしゃいませ。		Welcome./May I help you? (a greeting to a customer or a guest entering a shop, etc.)

◁会話▷

いい ［お］天気ですね。	Nice weather, isn't it?
お出かけですか。	Are you going out?
ちょっと ～まで。	I'm just going to ～.
行って いらっしゃい。	So long. (lit. Go and come back.)
行って まいります。	So long. (lit. I'm going and coming back.)
それから	and, furthermore

~~~~~~~~~~~~~~~~~~~~~~~~~~~~~~~~~~

オーストラリア	Australia

II. Translation

Sentence Patterns

1. There are seven tables in the meeting room.
2. I will stay in Japan for one year.

Example Sentences

1. How many apples did you buy?
   ···I bought four.

2. Give me five 80-yen stamps and two postcards, please.
   ···Certainly. That's 500 yen in all.

3. Are there foreign teachers at Fuji University?
   ···Yes, there are three. They are all Americans.

4. How many people are there in your family?
   ···There are five. My parents, my elder sister, my elder brother and me.

5. How many times a week do you play tennis?
   ···I play it about twice a week.

6. How long did you study Spanish, Mr. Tanaka?
   ···I studied it for three months.
   Only three months? You speak it very well.

7. How long does it take from Osaka to Tokyo by Shinkansen?
   ···It takes two and a half hours.

Conversation

Please send this by sea mail

Janitor:	Nice weather, isn't it? Are you going out?
Wang:	Yes, I am going to the post office.
Janitor:	Really? See you later.
Wang:	See you.

Wang:	I would like to send this by special delivery.
Post office clerk:	Sure. To Australia? That's 370 yen.
Wang:	And also this parcel.
Post office clerk:	By sea mail or airmail?
Wang:	How much is sea mail?
Post office clerk:	500 yen.
Wang:	How long will it take?
Post office clerk:	It will take about one month.
Wang:	Well, please send it by sea mail.

III. Reference Words & Information

メニュー　　MENU

定食	set meal
ランチ	set meal in the western style
天どん	a bowl of rice with fried fish and vegetables
親子どん	a bowl of rice with chicken and egg
牛どん	a bowl of rice with beef
焼肉	grilled meat
野菜いため	sauteed vegetables
漬物	pickles
みそ汁	miso soup
おにぎり	rice ball
てんぷら	fried seafood and vegetables
すし	vinegared rice with raw fish
うどん	Japanese noodles made from wheat flour
そば	Japanese noodles made from buckwheat flour
ラーメン	Chinese noodles in soup with meat and vegetables
焼きそば	Chinese stir-fried noodles with pork and vegetables
お好み焼き	a type of pancake grilled with meat, vegetables and egg

カレーライス	curry and rice
ハンバーグ	hamburg steak
コロッケ	croquette
えびフライ	fried shrimp
フライドチキン	fried chicken
サラダ	salad
スープ	soup
スパゲティー	spaghetti
ピザ	pizza
ハンバーガー	hamburger
サンドウィッチ	sandwich
トースト	toast
コーヒー	coffee
紅茶	black tea
ココア	cocoa
ジュース	juice
コーラ	cola

IV. Grammar Explanation

1. Saying numbers

1) ひとつ, ふたつ……とお

These words are used to count things up to ten. Eleven and higher are counted by using the numbers themselves.

2) Counter Suffixes

When counting some sorts of things or expressing the quantity of things, counter suffixes are attached after the numbers.

一人	number of people except for one and two
	ひとり（1人）and ふたり（2人）are used for one and two. 4人 (four people) is read よにん.
一台	number of machines or vehicles like cars and bicycles
一枚	number of thin or flat things such as paper, dishes, shirts, CDs, etc.
一回	times
一分	minutes
一時間	hours
一日	days
	The number of days takes the counter suffix にち. However, from two to ten, the same words as used for dates are used. ("One day" is 1にち, "two days" is ふつか, ……, "ten days" is とおか.)
一週間	weeks
一か月	months
一年	years

Details and other counter suffixes are listed in the appendices.

3) Usage

Quantifiers (numbers with counter suffixes) are usually put before the verbs they modify. However, this is not always the case with length of time.

① りんごを 4つ 買いました。　　　We bought four apples.

② 外国人の 学生が 2人 います。　　There are two foreign students.

③ 国で 2か月 日本語を 勉強しました。

I studied Japanese for two months in my country.

4) Interrogatives

(1) いくつ is used to ask how many about things which are counted as ひとつ, ふたつ, …….

④ みかんを いくつ 買いましたか。

…8つ 買いました。

How many mandarin oranges did you buy?

…I bought eight.

(2) なん is used with a counter suffix to ask how many.

⑤ この　会社に　外国人が　何人　いますか。

…5人　います。

How many foreigners are there in this company?

…There are five.

⑥ 毎晩　何時間　日本語を　勉強しますか。

…2時間　勉強します。

How many hours do you study Japanese every night?

…Two hours.

(3) どのくらい is used to ask the length of time something takes. You can use various units of time in the answer.

⑦ どのくらい　日本語を　勉強しましたか。

…3年　勉強しました。

How long did you study Japanese?

…I studied it for three years.

⑧ 大阪から　東京まで　どのくらい　かかりますか。

…新幹線で　2時間半　かかります。

How long does it take from Osaka to Tokyo?

…It takes two and a half hours by Shinkansen.

5) ぐらい

ぐらい is added after quantifiers to mean "about."

⑨ 学校に　先生が　30人ぐらい　います。

There are about thirty teachers in our school.

⑩ 15分ぐらい　かかります。　　　　　It takes about fifteen minutes.

2. Quantifier (period) に －回 V

With this expression you can say how often you do something.

⑪ 1か月に　2回　映画を　見ます。　　I go to see movies twice a month.

3. Quantifier だけ／N だけ

だけ means "only." It is added after quantifiers or nouns to express that there is no more or nothing (no one) else.

⑫ パワー電気に　外国人の　社員が　1人だけ　います。

There is only one foreign employee in Power Electric.

⑬ 休みは　日曜日だけです。　　　　　I only have Sundays off.

Lesson 12

I. Vocabulary

かんたん［な］	簡単［な］	easy, simple
ちかい	近い	near
とおい	遠い	far
はやい	速い、早い	fast, early
おそい	遅い	slow, late
おおい	多い	many [people], much
［ひとが～］	［人が～］	
すくない	少ない	few [people], a little
［ひとが～］	［人が～］	
あたたかい	暖かい、温かい	warm
すずしい	涼しい	cool
あまい	甘い	sweet
からい	辛い	hot (taste), spicy
おもい	重い	heavy
かるい	軽い	light
いい		prefer [coffee]
［コーヒーが～］		
きせつ	季節	season
はる	春	spring
なつ	夏	summer
あき	秋	autumn, fall
ふゆ	冬	winter
てんき	天気	weather
あめ	雨	rain, rainy
ゆき	雪	snow, snowy
くもり	曇り	cloudy
ホテル		hotel
くうこう	空港	airport
うみ	海	sea, ocean
せかい	世界	world

パーティー		party (〜を します: give a party)
［お］まつり	［お］祭り	festival
しけん	試験	examination
すきやき	すき焼き	sukiyaki (beef and vegetable hot pot)
さしみ	刺身	sashimi (sliced raw fish)
［お］すし		sushi (vinegared rice topped with raw fish)
てんぷら		tempura (seafood and vegetables deep fried in batter)
いけばな	生け花	flower arrangement (〜を します: practice flower arrangement)
もみじ	紅葉	maple, red leaves of autumn
どちら		which one (between two things)
どちらも		both
ずっと		by far
はじめて	初めて	for the first time

◁会話▷

ただいま。	I'm home.
お帰りなさい。	Welcome home.
すごいですね。	That's amazing.
でも	but
疲れました。	(I'm) tired.

~~~~~~~~~~~~~~~~~~~~~~~~~~~~~~~~~~~~

祇園祭	the Gion Festival, the most famous festival in Kyoto
ホンコン	Hong Kong (香港)
シンガポール	Singapore
毎日屋	fictitious supermarket
ABCストア	fictitious supermarket
ジャパン	fictitious supermarket

II. Translation

Sentence Patterns

1. It was rainy yesterday.
2. It was cold yesterday.
3. Hokkaido is bigger than Kyushu.
4. I like summer best of the year.

Example Sentences

1. Was Kyoto quiet?
   ···No, it wasn't.

2. Was the trip enjoyable?
   ···Yes, it was very enjoyable.

3. Was the weather good?
   ···No, it wasn't so good.

4. How was the party yesterday?
   ···It was very lively. I met various people.

5. Are there more people in Tokyo than in New York?
   ···Yes, a lot more.

6. Which is the faster way to get to the airport, by bus or by train?
   ···The train is faster.

7. Which do you prefer, the sea or the mountains?
   ···I like both.

8. What do you like best of all Japanese dishes?
   ···I like tempura best.

Conversation

How was the Festival?

Miller:	Hello. (I'm home.)
Janitor:	Hello. (Welcome home.)
Miller:	This is a souvenir from Kyoto.
Janitor:	Thank you.
	How was the Gion Festival?
Miller:	It was very interesting.
	There were a lot of foreign visitors.
Janitor:	The Gion Festival is the most famous of all the festivals in Kyoto.
Miller:	Is that so?
Janitor:	Did you take photos?
Miller:	Yes, I took about a hundred photos.
Janitor:	Amazing!
Miller:	Yes. But it made me a bit tired.

III. Reference Words & Information

祭りと名所　FESTIVALS & PLACES OF NOTE

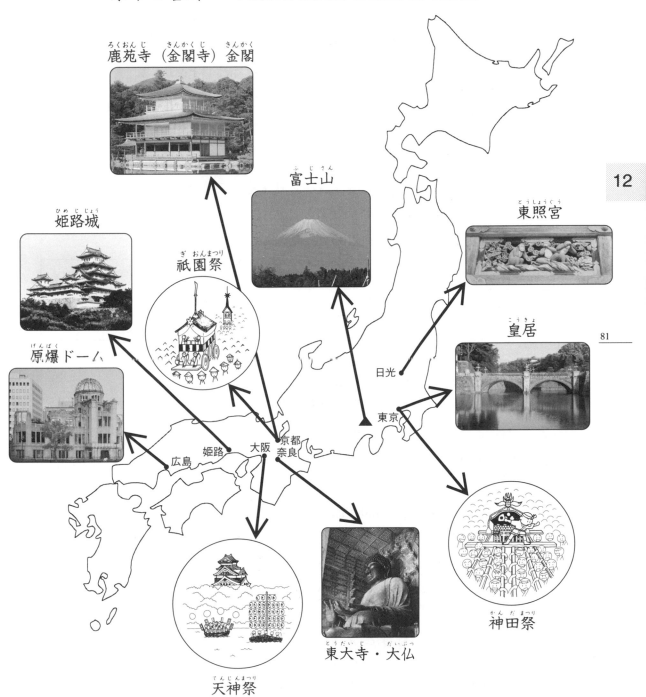

鹿苑寺（金閣寺）金閣

姫路城

祇園祭

富士山

東照宮

原爆ドーム

皇居

日光

東京

広島　姫路　大阪　京都　奈良

天神祭

東大寺・大仏

神田祭

IV. Grammar Explanation

1. Past tense of noun sentences and な-adjective sentences

	non-past (present/future)		past	
affirmative	N な-adj	あめ しずか } です	N な-adj	あめ しずか } でした
negative	N な-adj	あめ しずか } じゃ ありません (では)	N な-adj	あめ しずか } じゃ ありませんでした (では)

① きのうは 雨でした。　　　　　　　It was rainy yesterday.
② きのうの 試験は 簡単じゃ ありませんでした。
　　Yesterday's exam was not easy.

2. Past tense of い-adjective sentences

	non-past (present/future)	past
affirmative	あついです	あつかったです
negative	あつくないです	あつくなかったです

③ きのうは 暑かったです。　　　　It was hot yesterday.
④ きのうの パーティーは あまり 楽しくなかったです。
　　I didn't enjoy yesterday's party very much.

3. | N₁は N₂より adjective です |

This sentence pattern describes the quality and/or state of N₁ in comparison with N₂.
⑤ この 車は あの 車より 大きいです。
　　This car is bigger than that car.

4. | N₁と N₂と どちらが adjective ですか |
| …N₁/N₂ の ほうが adjective です |

The question asks the listener to choose between two items (N₁ and N₂). The interrogative used is always どちら if the comparison is made between two items.
⑥ サッカーと 野球と どちらが おもしろいですか。
　　…サッカーの ほうが おもしろいです。
　　Which is more interesting, baseball or football?
　　…Football is.

⑦ ミラーさんと サントスさんと どちらが テニスが 上手ですか。

Who is a better tennis player, Mr. Miller or Mr. Santos?

⑧ 北海道と 大阪と どちらが 涼しいですか。

Which is cooler, Hokkaido or Osaka?

⑨ 春と 秋と どちらが 好きですか。

Which do you like better, spring or autumn?

5.

| N₁ [の 中]で | 何 / どこ / だれ / いつ | が いちばん **adjective** ですか |

　　…N₂が いちばん **adjective** です

This question pattern is used to ask the listener to choose something that is the most "adjective." The choice is made from the group or category denoted by N₁. The interrogative used is decided by the kind of category from which the choice is made.

⑩ 日本料理[の 中]で 何が いちばん おいしいですか。

　…てんぷらが いちばん おいしいです。

Among Japanese dishes, what is the most delicious?

　…Tempura is.

⑪ ヨーロッパで どこが いちばん よかったですか。

　…スイスが いちばん よかったです。

In Europe, where did you like best?

　…I liked Switzerland best.

⑫ 家族で だれが いちばん 背が 高いですか。

　…弟が いちばん 背が 高いです。

Who is the tallest of your family?

　…My younger brother is.

⑬ 1年で いつが いちばん 寒いですか。

　…2月が いちばん 寒いです。

When is the coldest time of a year?

　…It's coldest in February.

[Note] When the subject is an interrogative, the particle が is used. (See Lesson 10, なにが ありますか／だれが いますか.)

When the subject of an adjective sentence is questioned, が is attached to the interrogative in the same way.

Lesson 13

I.   Vocabulary

あそびます	遊びます	enjoy oneself, play
およぎます	泳ぎます	swim
むかえます	迎えます	go to meet, welcome
つかれます	疲れます	get tired
だします	出します	send [a letter]
[てがみを ～]	[手紙を ～]	
はいります	入ります	enter [a coffee shop]
[きっさてんに ～]	[喫茶店に ～]	
でます	出ます	go out [of a coffee shop]
[きっさてんを ～]	[喫茶店を ～]	
けっこんします	結婚します	marry, get married
かいものします	買い物します	do shopping
しょくじします	食事します	have a meal, dine
さんぽします	散歩します	take a walk [in a park]
[こうえんを ～]	[公園を ～]	

たいへん [な]	大変 [な]	hard, tough, severe, awful
ほしい	欲しい	want (something)
さびしい	寂しい	lonely
ひろい	広い	wide, spacious
せまい	狭い	narrow, small (room, etc.)
しゃくしょ	市役所	municipal office, city hall
プール		swimming pool
かわ	川	river
けいざい	経済	economy
びじゅつ	美術	fine arts
つり	釣り	fishing (～を します: fish, angle)
スキー		skiing (～を します: ski)
かいぎ	会議	meeting, conference (～を します: hold a conference)
とうろく	登録	registration (～を します: register)

しゅうまつ	週末	weekend
～ごろ		about (time)
なにか	何か	something
どこか		somewhere, some place
おなかが すきました。		(I'm) hungry.
おなかが いっぱいです。		(I'm) full.
のどが かわきました。		(I'm) thirsty.
そうですね。		I agree with you.
そう しましょう。		Let's do that. (used when agreeing with someone's suggestion)

◁会話▷

ご注文は？	May I take your order?
定食	set meal
牛どん	bowl of rice topped with beef
[少々] お待ちください。	Please wait [a moment].
別々に	separately

〜〜〜〜〜〜〜〜〜〜〜〜〜〜〜〜〜〜〜〜〜〜〜

ロシア	Russia
つるや	fictitious Japanese restaurant
おはようテレビ	fictitious TV program

II. Translation

Sentence Patterns

1. I want a personal computer.
2. I want to eat tempura.
3. I will go to France to study cooking.

Example Sentences

1. What do you want most now?
    ···I want a house.

2. Where do you want to go on summer vacation?
    ···I want to go to Okinawa.

3. Because I am tired today, I don't want to do anything.
    ···Me, too. Today's meeting was tough, wasn't it?

4. What will you do this weekend?
    ···I will go to Kobe with my children to see the ships.

5. What did you come to Japan to study?
    ···I came here to study economics.

6. Did you go anywhere on winter vacation?
    ···Yes, I did.
    Where did you go?
    ···I went to Hokkaido to ski.

Conversation

Charge us separately

Yamada:	Why, it's already twelve. Shall we go for lunch?
Miller:	Sure.
Yamada:	Where shall we go?
Miller:	Let me see. Today I want to eat Japanese food.
Yamada:	Then, let's go to "Tsuru-ya."

Waiter:	May I take your order?
Miller:	I'll have the tempura set lunch.
Yamada:	I'll have the gyudon.
Waiter:	One tempura set lunch and one gyudon. I'll be right back.

Cashier:	1,680 yen altogether, sir.
Miller:	Excuse me. Please charge us separately.
Cashier:	Right. 980 yen for the tempura set lunch, 700 yen for the gyudon.

III. Reference Words & Information

町の中   TOWN

博物館	museum
美術館	art museum
図書館	library
映画館	movie theater
動物園	zoo
植物園	botanical garden
遊園地	amusement park
お寺	Buddhist temple
神社	Shinto shrine
教会	Christian church
モスク	Mosque
体育館	gymnasium
プール	swimming pool
公園	park
大使館	embassy
入国管理局	immigration bureau

市役所	city hall
警察署	police
交番	police box
消防署	fire station
駐車場	parking lot
大学	university
高校	senior high school
中学校	junior high school
小学校	elementary school
幼稚園	kindergarten
肉屋	butcher's shop
パン屋	bakery
魚屋	fishmonger's
酒屋	liquor shop
八百屋	vegetable shop
喫茶店	coffee shop
コンビニ	convenience store
スーパー	supermarket
デパート	department store

KOBAN

IV. Grammar Explanation

1. ┌ N が 欲しいです ┐

This sentence pattern is used to express the speaker's desire to possess or have an object. It can also be used to ask what the listener wants. The object is marked with the particle が. ほしい is an い-adjective.

① わたしは 友達が 欲しいです。　　　I want a friend.

② 今 何が いちばん 欲しいですか。　　What do you want most now?

　…車が 欲しいです。　　　　　　　…I want a car most.

③ 子どもが 欲しいですか。　　　　　Do you want a child?

　…いいえ、欲しくないです。　　　　…No, I don't.

2. ┌ V ます-form たいです ┐

1) Verb ます-form

The form of a verb when it is used with ます is called the ます-form. In the word かいます, かい is the ます-form.

2) V ます-form たいです

This expresses the speaker's desire to do something. It is also used to ask what the listener wants to do. In this expression, as is seen in ⑤ below, the particle が can replace the particle を. The other particles cannot be replaced by が. V ます-form たい inflects as an い-adjective.

④ わたしは 沖縄へ 行きたいです。　　I want to go to Okinawa.

⑤ わたしは てんぷらを 食べたいです。I want to eat tempura.
　　　　　　　　　(が)

⑥ 神戸で 何を 買いたいですか。　　What do you want to buy in Kobe?
　　　　　(が)

　…靴を 買いたいです。　　　　　　…I want to buy a pair of shoes.
　　　(が)

⑦ おなかが 痛いですから、何も 食べたくないです。

　　Because I have a stomachache, I don't want to eat anything.

[Note 1] ほしいです or 〜たいです cannot be used to describe the third person's desire.

[Note 2] You can neither use ほしいですか nor V ます-form たいですか when you offer something or invite someone to do something. For example, when you offer a cup of coffee (or invite the listener to have a cup of coffee), you should not say, コーヒーが ほしいですか, nor should you say コーヒーを のみたいですか. Expressions such as コーヒーは いかがですか or コーヒーを のみませんか should be used.

3.

$$\text{N (place) へ} \left\{ \begin{array}{l} \text{V ます-form} \\ \text{N} \end{array} \right\} \text{に 行きます／来ます／帰ります}$$

The purpose for いきます, きます or かえります is expressed using this pattern. The purpose is marked with the particle に. A noun used before に is of the kind denoting an action.

⑧ 神戸へ インド料理を 食べに 行きます。

I'm going to Kobe to eat Indian food.

⑨ 神戸へ 買い物に 行きます。

I'm going to Kobe for shopping.

⑩ 日本へ 美術の 勉強に 来ました。

I came to Japan in order to study art.

[Note] You can also use nouns denoting events such as festivals and concerts before に. In this case, the speaker's purpose is to see or enjoy the event.

⑪ あした 京都の お祭りに 行きます。

I'll go to the festival in Kyoto tomorrow.

4. N に V／N を V

The particle に marks the goal when used with verbs like はいります, のります (get on; see Lesson 16), etc. The particle を marks the starting point or place when used with verbs like でます, おります (get off; see Lesson 16), etc.

⑫ あの 喫茶店に 入りましょう。 Let's go in that coffee shop.

⑬ 7時に うちを 出ます。 I leave my house at 7 o'clock.

5. どこか／何か

どこか means anywhere or somewhere. なにか means anything or something. The particles へ and を can be omitted.

⑭ 冬休みは どこか[へ] 行きましたか。

…はい、行きました。

Did you go anywhere in the winter vacation?

…Yes, I did.

⑮ のどが かわきましたから、何か[を] 飲みたいです。

I'm thirsty. I want to drink something.

6. ご注文

ご is a prefix added to some words to express respect.

⑯ ご注文は？ May I have your order?

Lesson 14

I. Vocabulary

つけます II		turn on
けします I	消します	turn off
あけます II	開けます	open
しめます II	閉めます	close, shut
いそぎます I	急ぎます	hurry
まちます I	待ちます	wait
とめます II	止めます	stop, park
まがります I	曲がります	turn [to the right]
[みぎへ ～]	[右へ ～]	
もちます I	持ちます	hold
とります I	取ります	take, pass
てつだいます I	手伝います	help (with a task)
よびます I	呼びます	call
はなします I	話します	speak, talk
みせます II	見せます	show
おしえます II	教えます	tell [an address]
[じゅうしょを ～]	[住所を ～]	
はじめます II	始めます	start, begin
ふります I	降ります	rain
[あめが ～]	[雨が ～]	
コピーします III		copy
エアコン		air conditioner
パスポート		passport
なまえ	名前	name
じゅうしょ	住所	address
ちず	地図	map
しお	塩	salt
さとう	砂糖	sugar
よみかた	読み方	how to read, way of reading
～かた	～方	how to ～, way of ～ ing

ゆっくり		slowly, leisurely
すぐ		immediately
また		again
あとで		later
もう すこし	もう 少し	a little more
もう 〜		〜 more, another 〜

いいですよ。	Sure./Certainly.
さあ	right (used when encouraging some course of action)
あれ？	Oh! (in surprise or in wonder)

◁会話▷

信号を 右へ 曲がって ください。	Turn to the right at the signal.
まっすぐ	straight
これで お願いします。	I'd like to pay with this.
お釣り	change

〜〜〜〜〜〜〜〜〜〜〜〜〜〜〜〜〜〜〜〜〜〜〜

梅田	name of a town in Osaka

14

II. Translation

Sentence Patterns

1. Wait a moment, please.
2. Mr. Miller is making a telephone call now.

Example Sentences

1. Please write your name and address here.
   ···Yes.

2. Please show me that shirt.
   ···Here you are.
   Do you have one a little bigger?
   ···Yes. How about this shirt?

3. Excuse me. Please tell me how to read this kanji.
   ···It's "kakitome."

4. It's hot, isn't it? Shall I open the window?
   ···Yes, please.

5. Shall I come to the station to pick you up?
   ···No, thank you. I will come by taxi.

6. Where is Ms. Sato?
   ···She is talking with Mr. Matsumoto in the meeting room.
   Then, I will come again later.

Conversation

To Umeda, please

Karina:	To Umeda, please.
Driver:	Yes.

Karina:	Excuse me. Turn to the right at that traffic light.
Driver:	To the right?
Karina:	Yes.

Driver:	Go straight?
Karina:	Yes, go straight.

Karina:	Stop in front of that flower shop.
Driver:	Yes.
	1,800 yen, please.
Karina:	Here you are.
Driver:	That's 3,200 yen change. Thank you.

14

III. Reference Words & Information

駅　STATION

Japanese	English	Japanese	English
切符売り場	ticket office, ticket area	特急	super-express train
自動券売機	ticket machine	急行	express train
精算機	fare adjustment machine	快速	rapid service train
改札口	wicket, ticket barrier	準急	semi-express train
出口	exit	普通	local train
入口	entrance		
東口	east exit	時刻表	timetable
西口	west exit	～発	departing ～
南口	south exit	～着	arriving at ～
北口	north exit	［東京］行き	for [TOKYO]
中央口	central exit		
		定期券	commutation ticket, commuter pass
［プラット］ホーム	platform	回数券	coupon ticket
売店	kiosk	片道	one way
コインロッカー	coin locker	往復	round trip
タクシー乗り場	taxi stand		
バスターミナル	bus terminal		
バス停	bus stop		

IV. Grammar Explanation

1. Verb conjugation

Verbs in Japanese change their forms, i.e., they conjugate, and they are divided into three groups according to the type of conjugation. Depending on the following phrases, you can make sentences with various meanings.

2. Verb groups

1) Group I verbs

In the verbs of this group, the last sound of the ます-form is that of the い-line. (See Main Textbook, p. 2, "かなと拍.")

　　かきます　write　　のみます　drink

2) Group II verbs

In most of the verbs of this group, the last sound of the ます-form is that of the え-line, but in some verbs the last sound of the ます-form is that of the い-line.

　　たべます　eat　　みせます　show　　みます　see

3) Group III verbs

Verbs of this group include します and "noun denoting an action + します" as well as きます.

3. Verb て-form

The verb form which ends with て or で is called the て-form. How to make the て-form of a verb depends on which group the verb belongs to as explained below. (See Main Textbook, Lesson 14, p. 116, 練習 A 1.)

1) Group I　　　Depending on the last sound of the ます-form, the て-form of the verbs of this group is made as shown in the form table. (See Main Textbook, Lesson 14, 練習 A 1.) Note that the て-form of the verb いきます, いって, is an exception.

2) Group II　　　Attach て to the ます-form.

3) Group III　　　Attach て to the ます-form.

4. | V て-form ください | Please do...

This sentence pattern is used to ask, instruct or encourage the listener to do something. Naturally, if the listener is one's superior, this expression cannot be used for giving instructions to him/her. The sentences shown below are examples of asking, instructing and encouraging, respectively.

① すみませんが、この 漢字の 読み方を 教えて ください。

　　Excuse me, could you tell me how to read this kanji, please?

② ここに 住所と 名前を 書いて ください。

　　Please write your name and address here.

③ ぜひ 遊びに 来て ください。　　　Please come to my place. (L. 25)

When it is used to ask the listener to do something, すみませんが is often added before V て-form ください as in ①. This expression is politer than only saying V て-form ください.

5. | V て-form います | be V-ing

This sentence pattern indicates that a certain action or motion is in progress.

④ ミラーさんは 今 電話を かけて います。

    Mr. Miller is making a phone call now.

⑤ 今 雨が 降って いますか。   Is it raining now?

  …はい、降って います。   …Yes, it is.

  …いいえ、降って いません。   …No, it is not.

6. | V ます-form ましょうか | Shall I...?

This expression is used when the speaker is offering to do something for the listener.

⑥ A：あしたも 来ましょうか。   Shall I come tomorrow, too?

  B：ええ、10時に 来て ください。   …Yes, please come at ten.

⑦ A：傘を 貸しましょうか。   Shall I lend you an umbrella?

  B：すみません。お願いします。   …Yes, please.

⑧ A：荷物を 持ちましょうか。   Shall I carry your parcel?

  B：いいえ、けっこうです。   …No, thank you.

In the above example conversations, B demonstrates how to politely ask or instruct someone to do something (⑥), to accept an offer with gratitude (⑦) and to decline an offer politely (⑧).

7. | S₁ が、 S₂ | ..., but...

⑨ 失礼ですが、お名前は？

    Excuse me, but may I have your name? (L.1)

⑩ すみませんが、塩を 取って ください。Please pass me the salt.

You learned the conjunctive particle が in Lesson 8. In expressions such as しつれいですが or すみませんが, which are used as introductory remarks when speaking to someone, が, losing its original meaning, is used to connect two sentences lightly.

8. | N が V |

When describing a natural phenomenon, the subject is indicated by が.

⑪ 雨が 降って います。   It is raining.

Lesson 15

I. Vocabulary

たちます I	立ちます	stand up
すわります I	座ります	sit down
つかいます I	使います	use
おきます I	置きます	put
つくります I	作ります、造ります	make, produce
うります I	売ります	sell
しります I	知ります	get to know
すみます I	住みます	be going to live
けんきゅうします III	研究します	do research
しって います	知って います	know
すんで います	住んで います	live [in Osaka]
[おおさかに～]	[大阪に～]	

しりょう	資料	materials, data
カタログ		catalog
じこくひょう	時刻表	timetable

ふく	服	clothes
せいひん	製品	products
ソフト		software
せんもん	専門	speciality, field of study

はいしゃ	歯医者	dentist, dentist's
とこや	床屋	barber, barber's

プレイガイド		(theater) ticket agency

どくしん	独身	single, unmarried

◀会話▶
特_{とく}に　　　　　　　　　　　　especially
思_{おも}い出_だします I　　　　　　　remember, recollect
ご家_か族_{ぞく}　　　　　　　　　　your family
いらっしゃいます I　　　　be (honorific equivalent of います)
高_{こう}校_{こう}　　　　　　　　　　senior high school

〰〰〰〰〰〰〰〰〰〰〰〰〰〰〰〰〰〰

日本橋_{にっぽんばし}　　　　　　　　　name of a shopping district in Osaka

15

II. Translation

Sentence Patterns

1. You may take photographs.
2. Mr. Santos has a personal computer.

Example Sentences

1. May I keep this catalog?
   ⋯Sure, please do.

2. May I borrow this dictionary?
   ⋯I'm sorry, but... I'm using it now.

3. You must not play here.
   ⋯All right.

4. Do you know the phone number of the City Hall?
   ⋯No, I don't.

5. Where do you live, Ms. Maria?
   ⋯I live in Osaka.

6. Is Mr. Wang single?
   ⋯No, he is married.

7. What is your job?
   ⋯I am a teacher. I teach at Fuji University.
   Your speciality?
   ⋯It's Japanese fine art.

Conversation

Tell me about your family

Miller:	Today's movie was good, wasn't it?
Kimura:	Yes, it was. The father was particularly good, wasn't he?
Miller:	Yes. I was reminded of my family.
Kimura:	Were you? Tell me about your family, Mr. Miller.
Miller:	I have my parents and an elder sister.
Kimura:	Where do they live?
Miller:	My parents live near New York City.
	My sister is in London.
	How about your family, Ms. Kimura?
Kimura:	There are three of us. My father works for a bank.
	My mother teaches English at a high school.

III. Reference Words & Information

職業　OCCUPATIONS

会社員 company employee	公務員 civil servant	駅員 station clerk	銀行員 bank clerk	郵便局員 postman
店員 shop clerk	調理師 cook	理容師 barber 美容師 beautician	教師 teacher	弁護士 lawyer
研究者 research worker	医者／看護婦 doctor/nurse	運転手 driver	警察官 policeman	外交官 diplomat
政治家 politician	画家 painter	作家 author	音楽家 musician	建築家 architect
エンジニア engineer	デザイナー designer	ジャーナリスト journalist	歌手／俳優 singer/actor actress	スポーツ選手 athlete

15

99

IV. Grammar Explanation

1. ┌ V て-form も いいです ┐ You may do...

This expression is used to grant permission.

① 写真を 撮っても いいです。　　　　　You may take pictures.

To ask for permission, the question form of this sentence is used.

② たばこを 吸っても いいですか。　　　May I smoke?

How to answer such a question using the same sentence pattern is as follows. Note that an euphemistic answer is given when permission is not granted.

③ この カタログを もらっても いいですか。

…ええ、いいですよ。どうぞ。

…すみません。ちょっと。

May I have this catalogue?

…Yes. Here you are.

…Sorry. I'm afraid not.

2. ┌ V て-form は いけません ┐ You must not do...

This sentence pattern is used to express prohibition.

④ ここで たばこを 吸っては いけません。禁煙ですから。

You must not smoke here.　Because this is no-smoking area.

When you strongly wish to refuse permission to questions using the expression V て-form も いいですか, you answer いいえ、いけません, omitting V て-form は. This expression cannot be used by an inferior to a superior.

⑤ 先生、ここで 遊んでも いいですか。　　May we play here, Ma'am?

…いいえ、いけません。　　　　　　　　…No, you must not.

3. ┌ V て-form います ┐

In addition to the usage of V て-form います you learned in Lesson 14, it is also used in describing a certain continuing state which resulted from a certain action in the past.

⑥ わたしは 結婚して います。　　　　I'm married.

⑦ わたしは 田中さんを 知って います。　I know Mr. Tanaka.

⑧ わたしは 大阪に 住んで います。　　　I live in Osaka.

⑨ わたしは カメラを 持って います。　　I have a camera.

もって います means "be holding" and "possess" as well.

4. V て-form います

V て-form います is also used in describing a habitual action; that is, when the same action is repeatedly performed over a period of time.

Therefore, one's occupation can be expressed by this sentence pattern, like in ⑫ and ⑬. So if the question おしごとは なんですか is asked, this sentence pattern can be used to answer it.

⑩ IMCは コンピューターソフトを 作って います。

IMC makes computer software.

⑪ スーパーで フィルムを 売って います。

Supermarkets sell films.

⑫ ミラーさんは IMCで 働いて います。

Mr. Miller works for IMC.

⑬ 妹は 大学で 勉強して います。

My younger sister is studying at university.

5. 知りません

The negative form of しって います is しりません。

⑭ 市役所の 電話番号を 知って いますか。

…はい、知って います。

…いいえ、知りません。

Do you know the telephone number of the city hall?

…Yes, I do.

…No, I don't.

Lesson 16

I.   Vocabulary

のります I	乗ります	ride, get on [a train]
[でんしゃに 〜]	[電車に 〜]	
おります II	降ります	get off [a train]
[でんしゃを 〜]	[電車を 〜]	
のりかえます II	乗り換えます	change (trains, etc.)
あびます II	浴びます	take [a shower]
[シャワーを 〜]		
いれます II	入れます	put in, insert
だします I	出します	take out, withdraw
はいります I	入ります	enter [university]
[だいがくに 〜]	[大学に 〜]	
でます II	出ます	graduate from [university]
[だいがくを 〜]	[大学を 〜]	
やめます II		quit or retire from [a company], stop, give up
[かいしゃを 〜]	[会社を 〜]	
おします I	押します	push, press
わかい	若い	young
ながい	長い	long
みじかい	短い	short
あかるい	明るい	bright, light
くらい	暗い	dark
せが たかい	背が 高い	tall (referring to person)
あたまが いい	頭が いい	clever, smart
からだ	体	body
あたま	頭	head
かみ	髪	hair
かお	顔	face
め	目	eye
みみ	耳	ear
くち	口	mouth
は	歯	tooth
おなか		stomach
あし	足	leg, foot

サービス		service
ジョギング		jogging （〜を します: jog)
シャワー		shower
みどり	緑	green, greenery
［お］てら	［お］寺	Buddhist temple
じんじゃ	神社	Shinto shrine
りゅうがくせい	留学生	foreign student
〜ばん	〜番	number 〜
どうやって		in what way, how
どの 〜		which 〜 (used for three or more)
［いいえ、］まだまだです。		[No,] I still have a long way to go.

16

◀会話▶

お引き出しですか。	Are you making a withdrawal?
まず	first of all
キャッシュカード	cash dispensing card
暗証番号	personal identification number, PIN
次に	next, as a next step
金額	amount of money
確認	confirmation （〜します: confirm)
ボタン	button

~~~~~~

ＪＲ	Japan Railway
アジア	Asia
バンドン	Bandung (in Indonesia)
ベラクルス	Veracruz (in Mexico)
フランケン	Franken (in Germany)
ベトナム	Vietnam
フエ	Hue (in Vietnam)
大学前	fictitious bus stop

II. Translation

Sentence Patterns

1. In the morning I go jogging, take a shower and go to the office.
2. We dined at a restaurant after the concert was over.
3. The food is delicious in Osaka.
4. This personal computer is light and handy.

Example Sentences

1. What did you do yesterday?
   ···I went to the library and borrowed some books, and then met a friend.

2. How do you go to your university?
   ···I take a No. 16 bus from Kyoto Station and get off at Daigaku-mae.

3. What are you going to do after getting back to your country?
   ···I will work for my father's company.

4. Which person is Mr. Santos?
   ···He is that tall man with dark hair.

5. What kind of city is Nara?
   ···It is a quiet and beautiful city.

6. Who is that person?
   ···That is Ms. Karina. She is Indonesian, and an overseas student at Fuji University.

Conversation

Tell me how to use this machine

Maria:	Excuse me. Could you tell me how to use this machine?
Bank clerk:	You want to make a withdrawal?
Maria:	Yes.
Bank clerk:	Then, please push this button, first.
Maria:	Yes.
Bank clerk:	Do you have a cash card?
Maria:	Yes, here it is.
Bank clerk:	Put it in here, and enter the code number.
Maria:	Yes.
Bank clerk:	Next, enter the sum.
Maria:	Fifty thousand yen. Five...
Bank clerk:	Push this "Man" and "En." And then push this "Kakunin" button.
Maria:	Got it. Thank you very much.

III. Reference Words & Information

ATMの使い方　HOW TO WITHDRAW MONEY

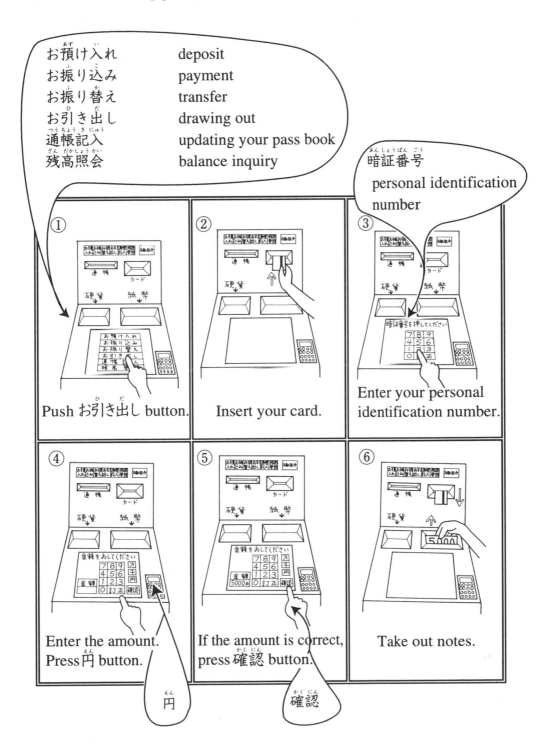

お預け入れ　deposit
お振り込み　payment
お振り替え　transfer
お引き出し　drawing out
通帳記入　updating your pass book
残高照会　balance inquiry

暗証番号　personal identification number

① Push お引き出し button.

② Insert your card.

③ Enter your personal identification number.

④ Enter the amount. Press 円 button.

⑤ If the amount is correct, press 確認 button.

⑥ Take out notes.

円

確認

IV. Grammar Explanation

1. V て-form、[V て-form]、～

To connect verb sentences, the て-form is used. When two or more actions take place in succession, the actions are mentioned in the order of occurrence by using the て-form. The tense of the sentence is determined by the tense form of the last verb in the sentence.

① 朝 ジョギングを して、シャワーを 浴びて、会社へ 行きます。

In the morning, I jog, take a shower and go to the office.

② 神戸へ 行って、映画を 見て、お茶を 飲みました。

I went to Kobe, saw a movie and drank tea.

2. い-adj (～い) → ～くて、～

When joining an い-adjective sentence to another sentence, take away the い from the い-adjective and attach くて.

おおき－い	→	おおき－くて	big
ちいさ－い	→	ちいさ－くて	small
いい－い	→	*よ－くて (exception)	good

③ ミラーさんは 若くて、元気です。

Mr. Miller is young and lively.

④ きのうは 天気が よくて、暑かったです。

Yesterday it was fine and hot.

3. N / な-adj [な] } で、～

When joining noun sentences or な-adjective sentences, です is changed to で.

⑤ カリナさんは インドネシア人で、京都大学の 留学生 です。

Ms. Karina is an Indonesian and a student of Kyoto University.

⑥ ミラーさんは ハンサムで、親切です。

Mr. Miller is handsome and kind.

⑦ 奈良は 静かで、きれいな 町です。

Nara is a quiet and beautiful city.

[Note 1] The above structures can be used not only for connecting sentences relating to the same topic but also sentences with different topics.

⑧ カリナさんは 学生で、マリアさんは 主婦です。

Ms. Karina is a student and Maria is a housewife.

[Note 2] This method cannot connect sentences of contradictory notion. In that case, が is used (see Lesson 8, 7).

× この 部屋は 狭くて、きれいです。

○ この 部屋は 狭いですが、きれいです。 This room is small but clean.

4. V₁ て-form から、V₂

This sentence pattern indicates that upon completion of the action denoted by V₁, the action of V₂ is to be conducted. The tense of the sentence is determined by the tense form of the last verb in the sentence.

⑨ 国へ 帰ってから、父の 会社で 働きます。

    I will work for my father's company after going back to my country.

⑩ コンサートが 終わってから、レストランで 食事しました。

    We ate at a restaurant after the concert was over.

[Note] The subject of a subordinate clause is indicated by が, as shown in the example sentence ⑩.

5. N₁ は N₂ が adjective

This sentence pattern is used to describe an attribute of a thing or a person. The topic of the sentence is denoted by は. N₁ is the topic of the sentence. N₂ is the subject of the adjective's description.

⑪ 大阪は 食べ物が おいしいです。   Food is tasty in Osaka.

⑫ ドイツの フランケンは ワインが 有名です。

    Franken in Germany produces famous wine.

⑬ マリアさんは 髪が 長いです。   Maria has long hair.

6. どうやって

どうやって is used to ask the way or the method of doing something. To answer such a question, the pattern learned in 1. is used.

⑭ 大学まで どうやって 行きますか。

    …京都駅から 16番の バスに 乗って、大学前で 降ります。

    How do you go to your university?

    …I take a No.16 bus from Kyoto Station and get off at Daigaku-mae.

7. どの N

You learned in Lesson 2 that この, その and あの modify nouns. The interrogative word used in this system is どの. どの is used to ask the listener to define one among more than two which are concretely presented.

⑮ サントスさんは どの 人 ですか。

    …あの 背が 高くて、髪が 黒い 人です。

    Which one is Mr. Santos?

    …That tall man with black hair is.

Lesson 17

I. Vocabulary

おぼえます II	覚えます	memorize
わすれます II	忘れます	forget
なくします I		lose
だします I	出します	hand in [a report]
[レポートを ～]		
はらいます I	払います	pay
かえします I	返します	give back, return
でかけます II	出かけます	go out
ぬぎます I	脱ぎます	take off (clothes, shoes, etc.)
もっていきます I	持って行きます	take (something)
もってきます III	持って来ます	bring (something)
しんぱいします III	心配します	worry
ざんぎょうします III	残業します	work overtime
しゅっちょうします III		go on a business trip
	出張します	
のみます I	飲みます	take [medicine]
[くすりを ～]	[薬を ～]	
はいります I	入ります	take [a bath]
[おふろに ～]		
たいせつ[な]	大切[な]	important, precious
だいじょうぶ[な]	大丈夫[な]	all right
あぶない	危ない	dangerous
もんだい	問題	question, problem, trouble
こたえ	答え	answer
きんえん	禁煙	no smoking
[けんこう]ほけんしょう		[health] insurance card
	[健康]保険証	
かぜ		cold, flu
ねつ	熱	fever
びょうき	病気	illness, disease
くすり	薬	medicine

［お］ふろ		bath
うわぎ	上着	jacket, outerwear
したぎ	下着	underwear
せんせい	先生	doctor (used when addressing a medical doctor)
２、３にち	２、３日	a few days
２、３〜		a few 〜 (〜 is a counter suffix)
〜までに		before 〜, by 〜 (indicating time limit)
ですから		therefore, so

◁会話▷

どう しましたか。	What's the matter?
［〜が］痛いです。	(I) have a pain [in my 〜].
のど	throat
お大事に。	Take care of yourself. (said to people who are ill)

II. Translation

Sentence Patterns

1. Please don't take photographs here.
2. You must show your passport.
3. You do not have to submit the report.

Example Sentences

1. Do not park your car there, please.
   ···I am sorry.

2. Doctor, may I drink alcohol?
   ···No, refrain from it for two or three days.
   Yes, doctor.

3. Shall we go for a drink tonight?
   ···Sorry. Today I'm going out with my wife.
   So I must go home early.

4. By when do I have to submit the report?
   ···Submit it by Friday, please.

5. Do the children have to pay, too?
   ···No, they don't have to pay.

Conversation

What seems to be the problem?

Doctor:	What seems to be the problem?
Matsumoto:	I have had a sore throat and a slight temperature since yesterday.
Doctor:	Well, please open your mouth.

Doctor:	You have a cold. You need a good rest.
Matsumoto:	Doctor, I have to go to Tokyo on business from tomorrow.
Doctor:	Well then, take this medicine and go to bed early today.
Matsumoto:	Yes, doctor.
Doctor:	And do not take a bath tonight.
Matsumoto:	I see.
Doctor:	Please take care.
Matsumoto:	Thank you very much, doctor.

III. Reference Words & Information

体・病気 BODY & ILLNESS

<small>からだ びょうき</small>

どう しましたか　What seems to be the problem?

頭が 痛い	have a headache
おなかが 痛い	have a stomachache
歯が 痛い	have a toothache
熱が ある	have a fever
せきが 出る	have a cough
鼻水が 出る	have a runny nose
血が 出る	bleed
吐き気が する	feel nauseous
寒気が する	feel a chill
めまいが する	feel dizzy
下痢を する	have diarrhea
便秘を する	be constipated
けがを する	get injured
やけどを する	get burnt
食欲が ない	have no appetite
肩が こる	feel stiff in one's shoulders
体が だるい	feel weary
かゆい	itchy

かお　あたま
め
はな　かみ
みみ
くち　のど　くび
あご　かた
むね　せなか
うで
ゆび　て　ひじ
つめ　ひざ　おなか　こし
ほね
あし　しり

111

かぜ	cold	ぎっくり腰	slipped disc
インフルエンザ	influenza	ねんざ	sprain
盲腸	appendicitis	骨折	bone fracture
		二日酔い	hangover

IV. Grammar Explanation

1. Verb ない-form

The verb form used with ない is called the ない-form; that is to say, かか of かかない is the ない-form of かきます (write). How to make the ない-form is given below (see Main Textbook, Lesson 17, p. 140, 練習 A 1).

1) Group I

In the verbs of this group the last sound of the ます-form is always the sound in the い-line. So, replace it with the sound of the あ-line to make a ない-form. The exceptions to this rule are such verbs as かいます, あいます, etc. (わ is the last sound of the ない-form in these verbs instead of あ.) (See Main Textbook, p. 2, "かなと拍.")

かき－ます → かか－ない		いそぎ－ます → いそが－ない	
よみ－ます → よま－ない		あそび－ます → あそば－ない	
とり－ます → とら－ない		まち－ます → また－ない	
すい－ます → すわ－ない		はなし－ます → はなさ－ない	

2) Group II

The ない-form of verbs of this group is just the same as the ます-form.

たべ－ます → たべ－ない
み－ます → み－ない

3) Group III

The ない-form of します is the same as the ます-form. きます becomes こ(ない).

べんきょうし－ます → べんきょうし－ない
し－ます → し－ない
き－ます → こ－ない

2. ┃ V ない-form ないで ください ┃ Please don't...

This expression is used to ask or instruct someone not to do something.

① わたしは 元気ですから、心配しないで ください。

I am fine, so please don't worry about me.

② ここで 写真を 撮らないで ください。

Please don't take pictures here.

3. ┃ V ない-form なければ なりません ┃ must...

This expression means something has to be done regardless of the will of the actor. Note that this doesn't have a negative meaning.

③ 薬を 飲まなければ なりません。　　I must take medicine.

4. | V ない-form なくても いいです | need not ...

This sentence pattern indicates that the action described by the verb does not have to be done.

④ あした 来なくても いいです。　　You don't have to come tomorrow.

5. | N (object) は |

You learned in Lesson 6 that the particle を is attached to the direct object of verbs. Here you learn that the object is made a topic by replacing を with は.

ここに 荷物を 置かないで ください。

Please don't put parcels here.

⑤ 荷物は ここに 置かないで ください。

As for parcels, don't put them here.

会社の 食堂で 昼ごはんを 食べます。

I have lunch in the company cafeteria.

⑥ 昼ごはんは 会社の 食堂で 食べます。

As for lunch, I have it in the company cafeteria.

6. | N (time) までに V |

The point in time indicated by までに is the time limit by which an action is to be done.

⑦ 会議は 5時までに 終わります。

The meeting will be over by five.

⑧ 土曜日までに 本を 返さなければ なりません。

I must return the book by Saturday.

[Note] Make sure you do not confuse までに with the particle まで.

5時まで 働きます。　　　　　　I work until five. (L. 4)

Lesson 18

I. Vocabulary

できます II		be able to, can
あらいます I	洗います	wash
ひきます I	弾きます	play (stringed instrument or piano, etc.)
うたいます I	歌います	sing
あつめます II	集めます	collect, gather
すてます II	捨てます	throw away
かえます II	換えます	exchange, change
うんてんします III	運転します	drive
よやくします III	予約します	reserve, book
けんがくします III	見学します	visit some place for study
ピアノ		piano
－メートル		－meter
こくさい～	国際～	international ～
げんきん	現金	cash
しゅみ	趣味	hobby
にっき	日記	diary
[お]いのり	[お]祈り	prayer (～を します: pray)
かちょう	課長	section chief
ぶちょう	部長	department chief
しゃちょう	社長	president of a company

◀会話▶

動物	animal
馬	horse
へえ	Really! (used when expressing surprise)
それは おもしろいですね。	That must be interesting.
なかなか	not easily (used with negatives)
牧場	ranch, stock farm
ほんとうですか。	Really?
ぜひ	by all means

〜〜〜〜〜〜〜〜〜〜〜〜〜〜〜〜〜〜〜〜〜〜〜〜〜〜

ビートルズ	the Beatles, famous British music group

18

II. Translation

Sentence Patterns

1. Mr. Miller can read Kanji.
2. My hobby is watching films.
3. I write in my diary before I go to bed.

Example Sentences

1. Can you ski?
   ⋯Yes, I can. But I am not very good at it.

2. Can you use a personal computer, Ms. Maria?
   ⋯No, I can't.

3. Until what time can we visit Osaka Castle?
   ⋯It is open until five o'clock.

4. Can I pay by credit card?
   ⋯I am sorry, but please pay in cash.

5. What is your hobby?
   ⋯Collecting old clocks and watches.

6. Must Japanese children learn Hiragana before they enter school?
   ⋯No, they need not.

7. Please take this medicine before meals.
   ⋯Yes, I will.

8. When did you get married?
   ⋯We got married three years ago.

Conversation

What is your hobby?

Yamada:	What is your hobby, Mr. Santos?
Santos:	Photography.
Yamada:	What kind of photos do you take?
Santos:	Photos of animals. I like those of horses, especially.
Yamada:	Oh, that's interesting.
	Have you taken photos of horses since you came to Japan?
Santos:	No.
	You can hardly ever see horses in Japan.
Yamada:	There is a lot of pastureland for horses in Hokkaido.
Santos:	Really?
	Then I would really like to go there on summer vacation.

III. Reference Words & Information

動き　ACTIONS

飛ぶ fly	跳ぶ jump	登る climb	走る run
泳ぐ swim	もぐる dive	飛び込む dive into	逆立ちする stand upside down
はう crawl	ける kick	振る wave	持ち上げる lift
投げる throw	たたく pat	引く pull	押す push
曲げる bend	伸ばす extend	転ぶ fall down	振り向く look back

IV. Grammar Explanation

1. Verb dictionary form

This form is the basic form of a verb. Verbs are given in this form in the dictionary, hence the name. How to make the dictionary form is given below. (See Main Textbook, Lesson 18, p. 148, 練習 A 1.)

1) Group Ⅰ   In the verbs of this group the last sound of the ます-form is always in the い-line. Replace it with the sound in the う-line to make the dictionary form. (See Main Textbook, p. 2, "かなと拍.")

2) Group Ⅱ   Attach る to the ます-form.

3) Group Ⅲ   します becomes する and きます becomes くる.

2.

N
V dictionary form こと } が できます	can...

できます is the verb which expresses ability or possibility. A noun and V dictionary form こと before が indicates the content of ability or possibility.

1) Noun

Nouns placed before が are mostly nouns which express actions such as driving a car, shopping, skiing, dancing, etc. Nouns such as にほんご, which is associated with the action はなす, or ピアノ, which is associated with the action ひく, can also be used here.

① ミラーさんは 日本語が できます。

　　　Mr. Miller can speak Japanese.

② 雪が たくさん 降りましたから、ことしは スキーが できます。

　　　It's snowed a lot, so we can ski this year.

2) Verb

When a verb is used to describe ability or possibility, こと should be attached to the dictionary form of the verb to make it a nominalized phrase and then が できます is put after that.

③ ミラーさんは 漢字を 読む ことが できます。

　　　　　　　　nominalized phrase　　　　Mr. Miller can read Kanji.

④ カードで 払う ことが できます。　　You can pay by credit card.

　　nominalized phrase

3.

わたしの 趣味は {	N
	V dictionary form こと } です	My hobby is...

As shown in ⑤ and ⑥ below, V dictionary form こと can express the content of hobbies more concretely than the noun alone can do.

⑤ わたしの 趣味は 音楽です。　　　　My hobby is music.

⑥ わたしの 趣味は 音楽を 聞く ことです。

　　My hobby is listening to the music.

4.
| V₁ dictionary form
N の
Quantifier (period) | まえに、V₂ | ..., before... |

1) Verb

This sentence pattern indicates that the action of V₂ occurs before the action of V₁ takes place. Even when the tense of V₂ is in the past tense or the future tense, V₁ is always in the dictionary form.

⑦ 日本へ 来る まえに、日本語を 勉強しました。

    I studied Japanese before I came to Japan.

⑧ 寝る まえに、本を 読みます。   I read a book before I go to bed.

2) Noun

When まえに comes after a noun, the particle の is put between the noun and まえに. Nouns before まえに are nouns which express actions or nouns which imply actions.

⑨ 食事の まえに、手を 洗います。   I wash my hands before eating.

3) Quantifier (period)

When まえに comes after a quantifier (period), the particle の is not necessary.

⑩ 田中さんは 1時間まえに、出かけました。

    Mr. Tanaka left an hour ago.

5. なかなか

When なかなか is accompanied by a negative expression, it means "not easily" or "not as expected."

⑪ 日本では なかなか 馬を 見る ことが できません。

    In Japan we can rarely see horses.

[Note] は of にほんでは in ⑪ is attached to で to emphasize the location or area under discussion.

6. ぜひ

ぜひ is used with expressions of hope and request such as ほしいです, V ます-form たいです and V て-form ください and emphasizes the meaning of the expressions.

⑫ ぜひ 北海道へ 行きたいです。

    I want to go to Hokkaido very much.

⑬ ぜひ 遊びに 来て ください。   Please come to my place. (L. 25)

Lesson 19

I. Vocabulary

のぼります I 　[やまに 〜]	登ります 　[山に 〜]	climb [a mountain]
とまります I 　[ホテルに 〜]	泊まります	stay [at a hotel]
そうじします Ⅲ	掃除します	clean (a room)
せんたくします Ⅲ	洗濯します	wash (clothes)
れんしゅうします Ⅲ	練習します	practice
なります I		become
ねむい	眠い	sleepy
つよい	強い	strong
よわい	弱い	weak
ちょうしが いい	調子が いい	be in good condition
ちょうしが わるい	調子が 悪い	be in bad condition
ちょうし	調子	condition
ゴルフ		golf (〜を します: play golf)
すもう	相撲	sumo wrestling
パチンコ		pinball game (〜を します: play pachinko)
おちゃ	お茶	tea ceremony
ひ	日	day, date
いちど	一度	once
いちども	一度も	not once, never (used with negatives)
だんだん		gradually
もうすぐ		soon
おかげさまで		Thank you. (used when expressing gratitude for help received)

◀会話▶

乾杯　　　　　　　　　Bottoms up./Cheers!
実は　　　　　　　　　actually, to tell the truth
ダイエット　　　　　　diet (〜を します: go on a diet)
何回も　　　　　　　　many times
しかし　　　　　　　　but, however
無理[な]　　　　　　　excessive, impossible
体に いい　　　　　　good for one's health
ケーキ　　　　　　　　cake

~~~~~~~~~~~~~~~~~~~~~~~~~~~~~~~

葛飾 北斎　　　　　　　famous Edo period wood block artist and
　　　　　　　　　　　painter (1760-1849)

19

II. Translation

Sentence Patterns

1. I have been to see sumo.
2. On holidays I play tennis, take walks and so on.
3. It's going to get hotter and hotter from now on.

Example Sentences

1. Have you been to Hokkaido?
   ···Yes, I once have. I went there two years ago with my friends.

2. Have you ever ridden a horse?
   ···No, I never have. I am eager to try it.

3. What did you do on your winter vacation?
   ···I visited temples and shrines in Kyoto, held a party with friends, and so on.

4. What would you like to do in Japan?
   ···I would like to go on a trip, learn the tea ceremony and so on.

5. How are you feeling?
   ···I've got better, thank you.

6. You have become good at Japanese.
   ···Thank you, but I still have a long way to go.

7. Teresa, what would you like to be?
   ···I would like to be a doctor.

Conversation

As for my diet, I'll start it tomorrow

All:	Cheers!

Ms. Matsumoto:	Why, Ms. Maria, you're not eating much.
Maria:	No. To tell the truth, I have been on a diet since yesterday.
Ms. Matsumoto:	Have you? I have tried being on a diet many times, too.
Maria:	What kind of diets have you tried?
Ms. Matsumoto:	I tried eating only apples, and drinking a lot of water, and so on.
Mr. Matsumoto:	I'm afraid strict diets are not good for your health.
Maria:	You are right.
Ms. Matsumoto:	Ms. Maria, this cake is delicious.
Maria:	Is it?
	.... I'll start dieting again tomorrow.

III. Reference Words & Information

伝統文化・娯楽　TRADITIONAL CULTURE & ENTERTAINMENT

茶道 tea ceremony（お茶）

華道 flower arrangement（生け花）

書道 calligraphy

歌舞伎 Kabuki

能 Noh

文楽 Bunraku

相撲 sumo

柔道 judo

剣道 kendo

空手 karate

漫才・落語 manzai, rakugo

囲碁・将棋 go, shogi

パチンコ pachinko

カラオケ karaoke

盆踊り Bon dance

123

IV. Grammar Explanation

1. Verb た-form

In this lesson you learn the た-form. How to make the た-form is shown below. (See Main Textbook, Lesson 19, p. 156, 練習 A 1.)

The た-form is made by changing て and で of the て-form into た and だ respectively.

	て-form	→	た-form
Group I	かいて	→	かいた
	のんで	→	のんだ
Group II	たべて	→	たべた
Group III	きて	→	きた
	して	→	した

2. | V た-form ことが あります |　have the experience of V-ing

This sentence pattern is used to describe what one has experienced in the past. This is basically the same sentence as わたしは N が あります which you learned in Lesson 9. The content of one's experience is expressed by the nominalized phrase V た-form こと.

① 馬に 乗った ことが あります。　　I have ridden a horse.

Note that it is, therefore, different from a sentence which merely states the fact that one did something at a certain time in the past.

② 去年 北海道で 馬に 乗りました。

　　I rode a horse in Hokkaido last year.

3. | V た-form り、 V た-form り します |　V ...and V ..., and so on

You learned an expression for referring to a few things and persons among many (〜や 〜[など]) in Lesson 10. The sentences learned here are used in referring to some actions among many other actions. The tense of this sentence pattern is shown at the end of the sentence.

③ 日曜日は テニスを したり、映画を 見たり します。

　　On Sundays I play tennis, see a movie and so on.

④ 日曜日は テニスを したり、映画を 見たり しました。

　　Last Sunday I played tennis, saw a movie and so on.

[Note] Make sure that you don't confuse the meaning of this sentence pattern with that of the て-form sentence (⑤) which you learned in Lesson 16.

⑤ 日曜日は テニスを して、映画を 見ました。

　　Last Sunday I played tennis and then saw a movie.

In ⑤ it is clear that seeing a movie took place after playing tennis. In ④ there is no time relation between the two activities. These activities are mentioned as example activities among the activities done on Sunday to imply that one did other activities besides them. And it is not natural that actions usually done by everybody every day such as getting up in the morning, taking meals, going to bed at night, etc., are mentioned.

4.

い-adj (〜い) → 〜く		
な-adj [な] → に	なります	become...
N に		

なります means "become" and indicates changes in a state or condition.

⑥ 寒い   →   寒く なります   get cold

⑦ 元気 [な]   →   元気に なります   get well

⑧ 25歳   →   25歳に なります   become 25 years old

5. そうですね

そうですね is used when you agree or sympathize with what your partner in conversation said. そうですか with a falling intonation is a similar expression to this (see Lesson 2, 6). そうですか(↘) is, however, an expression of your conviction or exclamation after getting information which was unknown to you, while そうですね is used to express your agreement or sympathy with your partner in conversation when he/she refers to something you agree with or already know.

⑨ 寒く なりましたね。   It's got cold, hasn't it?

　…そうですね。   …Yes, it has.

19

125

Lesson 20

I. Vocabulary

いります I 　[ビザが 〜]	要ります	need, require [a visa]
しらべます II	調べます	check, investigate
なおします I	直します	repair, correct
しゅうりします III	修理します	repair
でんわします III	電話します	phone
ぼく	僕	I (an informal equivalent of わたし used by men)
きみ	君	you (an informal equivalent of あなた used by men)
〜くん	〜君	Mr. (an informal equivalent of 〜さん used by men)
うん		yes (an informal equivalent of はい)
ううん		no (an informal equivalent of いいえ)
サラリーマン		salaried worker, office worker
ことば		word, language
ぶっか	物価	commodity prices
きもの	着物	kimono (traditional Japanese attire)
ビザ		visa
はじめ	初め	the beginning
おわり	終わり	the end
こっち		this way, this place (an informal equivalent of こちら)
そっち		this way, that place (an informal equivalent of そちら)
あっち		this way, that place over there (an informal equivalent of あちら)
どっち		which one (between two things), which way, where (an informal equivalent of どちら)

このあいだ	この間	the other day
みんなで		all together
〜けど		〜, but (an informal equivalent of が)

◁会話▷

国へ 帰るの？	Are you going back to your country?
どう するの？	What will you do?
どう しようかな。	What shall I do?
よかったら	if you like
いろいろ	various

II. Translation

Sentence Patterns

1. Mr. Santos did not come to the party.
2. Things are expensive in Japan.
3. The sea around Okinawa was beautiful.
4. Today is my birthday.

Example Sentences

1. Will you have some ice cream?
   ···Yes, I will.

2. Do you have any scissors?
   ···No, I don't.

3. Did you see Ms. Kimura yesterday?
   ···No, I didn't.

4. Shall we go to Kyoto all together tomorrow?
   ···Yes. That sounds nice.

5. Is the curry delicious?
   ···Yes, it is hot, but delicious.

6. Are you free now?
   ···Yes, I am. Why?
   Give me a hand, please.

7. Do you have a dictionary?
   ···No, I don't.

Conversation

What will you do for the summer vacation?

Kobayashi:	Are you going home for the summer vacation?
Thawaphon:	No, I won't. Though I want to....
	What about you, Mr. Kobayashi?
Kobayashi:	Well, what shall I do?
	Have you climbed Mt. Fuji, Mr. Thawaphon?
Thawaphon:	No, I haven't.
Kobayashi:	Then, if you'd like, shall we go together?
Thawaphon:	Yes, okay. When?
Kobayashi:	How about the beginning of August?
Thawaphon:	Sounds good.
Kobayashi:	Then, I will check up on various things and call you later.
Thawaphon:	Thanks. I'll be waiting.

Reference Words & Information

人の呼び方   HOW TO ADDRESS PEOPLE

"Taro, Hanako!!"

"Dear, do you know today is Taro's birthday?'

In families, people call each other from the viewpoint of the youngest of the family. A parent calls his/her eldest son or daughter "おにいちゃん" (elder brother) or "おねえちゃん" (elder sister) respectively, standing in the position of his/her younger sister or brother.

When parents talk in the presence of their children, the husband calls his wife "おかあさん" or "ママ" (mother), and the wife, her husband "おとうさん" or "パパ" (father). This practice, however, has been changing recently, and the number of couples who call each other by their names is increasing.

"Mr. Matsumoto, may I have your signature?"

"The necktie suits you very much, sir (ma'am)"

"Doctor, I have a stomachache."

In society, people call each other by the names of their role in the group to which they belong. At work, a subordinate calls his boss by his job title. At shops a shop assistant calls his/her customer "おきゃくさま" (Mr./Ms. customer). Doctors are called "せんせい" (teacher) by their patients.

IV. Grammar Explanation

1. Polite style and plain style

Japanese language has two styles of speech: polite style and plain style.

polite style	plain style
あした 東京へ 行きます。 I will go to Tokyo tomorrow.	あした 東京へ 行く。 I will go to Tokyo tomorrow.
毎日 忙しいです。 I am busy every day.	毎日 忙しい。 I am busy every day.
相撲が 好きです。 I like sumo.	相撲が 好きだ I like sumo.
富士山に 登りたいです。 I want to climb Mt. Fuji.	富士山に 登りたい。 I want to climb Mt. Fuji.
ドイツへ 行った ことが ありません。 I have never been to Germany.	ドイツへ 行った ことが ない。 I have never been to Germany.

The predicates which are used in polite style sentences and accompanied by either です or ます are called the polite form, while the predicates used in plain style sentences are called the plain form. (See Main Textbook, Lesson 20, p. 166, 練習 A 1)

2. Proper use of the polite style or the plain style

1) The polite style can be used at anytime in any place and to anybody. Therefore, the polite style is used most commonly in daily conversation between adults who are not close friends. It is used when talking to a person one has met for the first time, to one's superiors, or even to persons in a similar age group to whom one is not very close. The polite style may be chosen when one talks to a person who is younger or lower in rank yet not so close. The plain style is used when talking to one's close friends, colleagues and family members.
   Note that you need to be careful about how much politeness is needed, basing this on the age of your conversation partner and your type of relationship. If the plain style is used inappropriately, you could sound rough and impolite, so when you cannot tell the situation it is safer to use the polite style.

2) The plain style is commonly used in written work. Newspapers, books, theses and diaries are all written in the plain style. Most letters are written in the polite style.

3. Conversation in the plain style

1) Questions in the plain style generally omit the particle か, which denotes a question, and end with a rising intonation, such as のむ(↗).

① コーヒーを 飲む？（↗）   Do you want a coffee?
…うん、飲む。（↘）   …Yes, I do.

2) In noun and な-adjective questions, だ, which is the plain form of です, is omitted. In an answer in the affirmative, ending the sentence with だ could sound too rough. You can either omit だ or add some sentence final particle to soften the tone of the sentence. Women seldom use だ.

② 今晩 暇？   Are you free tonight?
                   (used by both men and women)
…うん、暇／暇だ／暇だよ。   …Yes, I am. (used by men)
…うん、暇／暇よ。   …Yes, I am. (used by women)
…ううん、暇じゃ ない。   …No, I am not.
                   (used by both men and women)

3) In the plain style, certain particles are often omitted if the meaning of the sentence is evident from the context.

③ ごはん [を] 食べる？   Will you take a meal?
④ あした 京都 [へ] 行かない？
     Won't you come to Kyoto tomorrow with me?
⑤ この りんご [は] おいしいね。   This apple is tasty, isn't it?
⑥ そこに はさみ [が] ある？   Is there a pair of scissors there?

で, に, から, まで, と, etc., however, are not omitted because the meaning of the sentence may not be clear without them.

4) In the plain style, い of V て-form いる is also often dropped.

⑦ 辞書、持って [い]る？   Do you have a dictionary?
…うん、持って [い]る。   … Yes, I do.
…ううん、持って [い]ない。   … No, I don't.

5) けど

けど has the same function as が, which is used to connect two sentences (see Lesson 8, 7 and Lesson 14, 7). It is often used in conversations.

⑧ その カレーライス [は] おいしい？
…うん、辛いけど、おいしい。
Is that curry and rice tasty?
…Yes, it's hot but tasty.
⑨ 相撲の チケット [が] あるけど いっしょに 行かない？
…いいね。
I have tickets for sumo. Won't you come with me.
…Sure.

Lesson 21

I.   Vocabulary

おもいます I	思います	think
いいます I	言います	say
たります II	足ります	be enough, be sufficient
かちます I	勝ちます	win
まけます II	負けます	lose, be beaten
あります I		[a festival] be held, take place
[おまつりが ～]	[お祭りが ～]	
やくに たちます I	役に 立ちます	be useful

むだ [な]		wasteful
ふべん [な]	不便 [な]	inconvenient

おなじ	同じ	the same

すごい		awful, great (expresses astonishment or admiration)

しゅしょう	首相	prime minister
だいとうりょう	大統領	president

せいじ	政治	politics
ニュース		news
スピーチ		speech (～を します: make a speech)
しあい	試合	game, match
アルバイト		side job (～を します: work part time)
いけん	意見	opinion
[お]はなし	[お]話	talk, speech, what one says, story (～を します: talk, tell a story)
ユーモア		humor
むだ		waste
デザイン		design

こうつう	交通	transportation, traffic
ラッシュ		rush hour

さいきん	最近	recently, these days
たぶん		probably, perhaps, maybe
きっと		surely
ほんとうに		really
そんなに		not so much (used with negatives)
〜に ついて		about 〜, concerning 〜
しかたが ありません。		There is no other choice./It can't be helped.

◁会話▷

しばらくですね。	It's been a long time (since I last saw you)./Long time no see.
〜でも 飲みませんか。	How about drinking 〜 or something?
見ないと……。	I've got to watch it.
もちろん	of course

~~~~~~~~~~~~~~~~~~~~~~~~~~~~~~~~~

カンガルー	kangaroo
キャプテン・クック	Captain James Cook (1728－79)

II. Translation

Sentence Patterns

1. I think it will rain tomorrow.
2. The prime minister said that he would go to the U.S.A. next month.

Example Sentences

1. Which is more important, work or family?
   ···I think both are important.

2. What do you think of Japan?
   ···I think things are expensive in Japan.

3. Where is Mr. Miller?
   ···I think he is in the meeting room.

4. Does Mr. Miller know this news?
   ···No, I don't think he does.
   He was on a business trip.

5. Has little Teresa fallen asleep yet?
   ···Yes, I think she has.

6. Do you pray before meals?
   ···No, we don't, but we say "Itadakimasu."

7. Did you say something in the meeting?
   ···Yes. I said that a lot of photocopying had been wastefully done.

8. In July there will be a festival in Kyoto, won't there?
   ···Yes, there will be.

Conversation

I think so, too

Matsumoto:	Mr. Santos, it's been a long time.
Santos:	Mr. Matsumoto, how are you?
Matsumoto:	I'm fine. How about going for a beer or something?
Santos:	That sounds good.

Santos:	There will be a soccer game between Japan and Brazil from ten tonight.
Matsumoto:	Yes, there will. I must be sure to watch it. Which team do you think will win?
Santos:	Of course, Brazil.
Matsumoto:	But I tell you recently Japan have got a lot better.
Santos:	I think so, too.... Oh, it's time that we went home.
Matsumoto:	Yes, it is. Let's go home.

III. Reference Words & Information

役職名 （やくしょくめい）　　POSITIONS IN SOCIETY

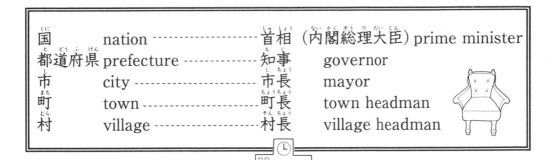

国（くに）　　nation ----------------- 首相（しゅしょう）（内閣総理大臣（ないかくそうりだいじん））prime minister
都道府県（とどうふけん）prefecture ------------- 知事（ちじ）　　governor
市（し）　　city -------------------- 市長（しちょう）　　mayor
町（まち）　　town ----------------- 町長（ちょうちょう）　town headman
村（むら）　　village ----------------- 村長（そんちょう）　village headman

大学（だいがく）　　university ------------- 学長（がくちょう）　president
高等学校（こうとうがっこう）senior high school --------
中学校（ちゅうがっこう）junior high school ------ 校長（こうちょう）　principal
小学校（しょうがっこう）elementary school -------
幼稚園（ようちえん）kindergarten ----------------- 園長（えんちょう）　director

会社（かいしゃ）　company

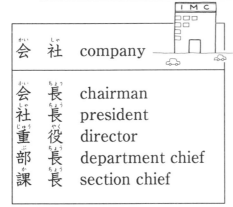

会長（かいちょう）　　chairman
社長（しゃちょう）　　president
重役（じゅうやく）　　director
部長（ぶちょう）　department chief
課長（かちょう）　section chief

銀行（ぎんこう）　bank

頭取（とうどり）　　president
支店長（してんちょう）branch manager

駅（えき）　　station

駅長（えきちょう）　stationmaster

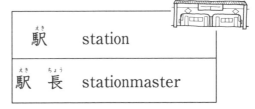

病院（びょういん）　hospital

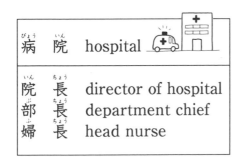

院長（いんちょう）　director of hospital
部長（ぶちょう）　department chief
婦長（ふちょう）　head nurse

警察（けいさつ）　police station

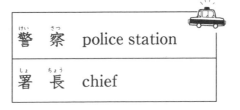

署長（しょちょう）　chief

IV. Grammar Explanation

1. | plain form と 思^{おも}います |　I think that...

The ideas or information expressed with おもいます are indicated by the particle と.

1) When expressing conjecture

① あした 雨^{あめ}が 降^ふると 思^{おも}います。　I think it will rain tomorrow.

② テレサちゃんは もう 寝^ねたと 思^{おも}います。

　　I think Teresa has already gone to bed.

When the content of conjecture is negative in nature, make the sentence before と negative.

③ ミラーさんは この ニュースを 知^しって いますか。

　　…いいえ、たぶん 知^しらないと 思^{おも}います。

　　Does Mr. Miller know this news?

　　…No, I don't think he does.

2) When expressing one's opinion

④ 日本^{にほん}は 物価^{ぶっか}が 高^{たか}いと 思^{おも}います。

　　I think that prices are high in Japan.

The expression 〜に ついて どう おもいますか is used to ask someone's opinion on something by using おもいます. と is not necessary after どう.

⑤ 新^{あたら}しい 空港^{くうこう}に ついて どう 思^{おも}いますか。

　　…きれいですが、ちょっと 交通^{こうつう}が 不便^{ふべん}だと 思^{おも}います。

　　What do you think of the new airport?

　　…I think that it is clean but the access to it is not easy.

Agreement or disagreement with other people's opinions can be expressed as follows.

⑥ A：ファクスは 便利^{べんり}ですね。

　 B：わたしも そう 思^{おも}います。

　 C：わたしは そう[は] 思^{おも}いません。

　 A：Fax machines are convenient, aren't they?

　 B：I think so, too.

　 C：I don't think so.

2. | "S" plain form } と 言^いいます |　say...

The content expressed with いいます is indicated by the particle と.

1) When quoting directly what someone says or said, repeat exactly what they say as in the following structure.

⑦ 寝^ねる まえに 「お休^{やす}みなさい」と 言^いいます。
　　We say "Good night" before going to bed.

⑧ ミラーさんは 「来週^{らいしゅう} 東京^{とうきょう}へ 出張^{しゅっちょう}します」と 言^いいました。
　　Mr. Miller said "I will go to Tokyo on a business trip next week."

21

2) When quoting indirectly what someone says or said, the plain form is used before と. The tense of the quoted sentence is not affected by the tense of the main sentence.

⑨ ミラーさんは 来週 東京へ 出張すると 言いました。
Mr. Miller said that he would go to Tokyo on a business trip next week.

3.

$$
\begin{array}{l}
\text{V} \\
\text{い-adj} \\
\text{な-adj} \\
\text{N}
\end{array}
\left.
\begin{array}{l}
\text{plain form} \\
\text{plain form} \\
\sim だ
\end{array}
\right\}
でしょう？
$$

When the speaker expects that the listener has some knowledge on the topic being discussed and that the listener will agree with the speaker's view, でしょう is said with a rising intonation to confirm the listener's agreement.

⑩ あした パーティーに 行くでしょう？
…ええ、行きます。

You are going to the party tomorrow, aren't you?
…Yes, I am.

⑪ 北海道は 寒かったでしょう？   It was cold in Hokkaido, wasn't it?
…いいえ、そんなに 寒くなかったです。   …No, it wasn't that cold.

4. N₁ (place)で N₂ が あります

When N₂ expresses such events as a party, concert, festival, incident, disaster and so on, あります means "to take place" or "to be held."

⑫ 東京で 日本と ブラジルの サッカーの 試合が あります。
A football game between Japan and Brazil will be held in Tokyo.

5. N(occasion)で

When some action takes place on a certain occasion, that occasion is followed by で.

⑬ 会議で 何か 意見を 言いましたか。
Did you give your opinion at the meeting?

6. Nでも V

でも is used to give an example out of things of the same kind (drinks in the case of ⑭) when one encourages or advises someone to do something or when one makes a suggestion.

⑭ ちょっと ビールでも 飲みませんか。
Shall we drink beer or something?

7. V ない-form ないと……

This expression is made by omitting いけません from V ない-form ないと いけません. V ない-form ないと いけません is similar to V ない-form なければ なりません which you learned in Lesson 17.

⑮ もう 帰らないと……。   I have to go home now.

137

Lesson 22

I.   Vocabulary

きます II [シャツを 〜]	着ます	put on [a shirt, etc.]
はきます I [くつを 〜]	[靴を 〜]	put on [shoes, trousers, etc.]
かぶります I [ぼうしを 〜]	[帽子を 〜]	put on [a hat, etc.]
かけます II [めがねを 〜]	[眼鏡を 〜]	put on [glasses]
うまれます II	生まれます	be born
コート		coat
スーツ		suit
セーター		sweater
ぼうし	帽子	hat, cap
めがね	眼鏡	glasses
よく		often
おめでとう ございます。		Congratulations. (used on birthdays, at weddings, New Year's Day, etc.)

◁会話▷

こちら	this (polite equivalent of これ)
家賃	house rent
うーん。	Let me see.
ダイニングキチン	kitchen with a dining area
和室	Japanese-style room
押し入れ	Japanese-style closet
布団	Japanese-style mattress and quilt
アパート	apartment

〜〜〜〜〜〜〜〜〜〜〜〜〜〜〜〜〜〜〜〜〜

パリ	Paris
万里の長城	the Great Wall of China
余暇開発センター	Center for Developing Leisure Activities
レジャー白書	white paper on leisure

II. Translation

Sentence Patterns

1. This is a cake Mr. Miller made.
2. That man who is over there is Mr. Miller.
3. I have forgotten the words I learned yesterday.
4. I have no time to go shopping.

Example Sentences

1. This is a photo I took on the Great Wall of China.
   ···Is it? It is superb, isn't it?

2. Which is the picture Ms. Karina drew?
   ···It is that one. That picture of the sea.

3. Who is that woman wearing the kimono?
   ···That is Ms. Kimura.

4. Mr. Yamada, where did you first meet your wife?
   ···It was Osaka Castle.

5. How was the concert you went to with Ms. Kimura?
   ···It was very good.

6. What's wrong with you?
   ···I have lost the umbrella I bought yesterday.

7. What kind of house do you want?
   ···I want a house that has a big garden.

8. Would you like to go for a drink this evening?
   ···I am sorry, but this evening I have promised to meet a friend.

Conversation

What kind of apartment would you like?

Real estate agent:	How about this one? The rent is 80,000 yen.
Wang:	Ummmm. It's far from the station.
Agent:	Then how about this one? This one's convenient. It's a three-minute walk from the station.
Wang:	Oh. A kitchen-dining room, a Japanese-style room, and.... Excuse me. What is this?
Agent:	It's an "oshiire." It's a place to put "futon" in.
Wang:	I see. Can I take a look at this apartment today?
Agent:	Yes. Shall we go now?
Wang:	Yes, please.

III. Reference Words & Information

衣服 CLOTHES

スーツ suit	ワンピース one-piece dress	上着 jacket	ズボン/パンツ trousers/pants ジーンズ jeans
スカート skirt	ブラウス blouse	ワイシャツ [white] shirt	セーター sweater
マフラー muffler 手袋 gloves	下着 underwear	くつした socks パンスト panty hose, tights	着物 kimono 帯 obi
オーバーコート overcoat レインコート raincoat	ネクタイ necktie ベルト belt	ハイヒール high heels ブーツ boots 運動靴 sneakers	ぞうり たび zori tabi

IV. Grammar Explanation

1. Noun modification

You learned how to modify nouns in Lesson 2 and Lesson 8.

ミラーさんの うち	Mr. Miller's house	(L. 2)
新しい うち	a new house	(L. 8)
きれいな うち	a beautiful house	(L. 8)

In Japanese, whatever modifies a word, whether it's a word or a sentence, it always comes before the word to be modified. Here you learn another way to modify nouns.

2. Noun modification by sentences

1) The predicate of the sentence which modifies a noun is in the plain form.

In the case of な-adjective sentences, 〜だ becomes 〜な. In the case of noun sentences 〜だ becomes 〜の.

① 京都へ { 行く 人 / 行かない 人 / 行った 人 / 行かなかった 人 }　　a person { who goes / who does not go / who went / who did not go } to Kyoto

背が 高くて、髪が 黒い 人　　a person who is tall and has black hair

親切で、きれいな 人　　a person who is kind and pretty

65歳の 人　　a person who is 65 years old

2) Nouns, which are various elements of the sentence, are picked out of it and can be modified by it.

② わたしは 先週 映画を 見ました → わたしが 先週 見た 映画

I saw a movie last week　　→the movie that I saw last week

③ ワンさんは 病院で 働いて います→ワンさんが 働いている 病院

Mr. Wang works at a hospital　　→the hospital where Mr. Wang works

④ わたしは あした 友達に 会います→わたしが あした 会う 友達

I will meet a friend tomorrow　　→the friend whom I will meet tomorrow

When the nouns underlined in ②, ③ and ④ are modified, the particles を, で, and に attached to them respectively are unnecessary.

22

142

3) The noun modified by a sentence ("the house where Mr. Miller lived" in the example sentences below) can be used in various parts of a sentence.

⑤ これは ミラーさんが 住んで いた うちです。

This is the house where Mr. Miller lived.

⑥ ミラーさんが 住んで いた うちは 古いです。

The house where Mr. Miller lived is old.

⑦ ミラーさんが 住んで いた うちを 買いました。

I bought the house where Mr. Miller lived.

⑧ わたしは ミラーさんが 住んで いた うちが 好きです。

I like the house where Mr. Miller lived.

⑨ ミラーさんが 住んで いた うちに 猫が いました。

There was a cat in the house where Mr. Miller lived.

⑩ ミラーさんが 住んで いた うちへ 行った ことが あります。

I have been to the house where Mr. Miller lived.

3. Nが

When a sentence modifies a noun, the subject in the sentence is indicated by が.

ミラーさんは ケーキを 作りました。
↓   Mr. Miller baked a cake.

⑪ これは ミラーさんが 作った ケーキです。

This is the cake which Mr. Miller baked.

⑫ わたしは カリナさんが かいた 絵が 好きです。

I like the picture that Ms. Karina drew.

⑬ [あなたは] 彼が 生まれた 所を 知って いますか。

Do you know the place where he was born?

4. V dictionary form 時間／約束／用事

When expressing the time for doing some activity, put the dictionary form of the action before じかん.

⑭ わたしは 朝ごはんを 食べる 時間が ありません。

I have no time to eat breakfast.

You can also say the content of the arrangement (appointment), etc., by putting the dictionary form of that action before やくそく, etc.

⑮ わたしは 友達と 映画を 見る 約束が あります。

I have an arrangement to see a movie with a friend of mine.

⑯ きょうは 市役所へ 行く 用事が あります。

I have something to do at the city hall today.

Lesson 23

I. Vocabulary

ききます I [せんせいに 〜]	聞きます [先生に 〜]	ask [the teacher]
まわします I	回します	turn
ひきます I	引きます	pull
かえます II	変えます	change
さわります I [ドアに 〜]	触ります	touch [a door]
でます II [おつりが 〜]	出ます [お釣りが 〜]	[change] come out
うごきます I [とけいが 〜]	動きます [時計が 〜]	[a watch] move, work
あるきます I [みちを 〜]	歩きます [道を 〜]	walk [along a road]
わたります I [はしを 〜]	渡ります [橋を 〜]	cross [a bridge]
きを つけます II [くるまに 〜]	気を つけます [車に 〜]	pay attention [to cars], take care
ひっこしします III	引っ越しします	move (house)
でんきや	電気屋	electrician
〜や	〜屋	person of 〜 shop
サイズ		size
おと	音	sound
きかい	機械	machine
つまみ		knob
こしょう	故障	breakdown (〜します：break down)
みち	道	road, way
こうさてん	交差点	crossroad
しんごう	信号	traffic light
かど	角	corner
はし	橋	bridge
ちゅうしゃじょう	駐車場	parking lot, car park

－め	－目	the -th (indicating order)
［お］しょうがつ	［お］正月	New Year's Day
ごちそうさま［でした］。		That was delicious. (said after eating or drinking)

◁会話▷

建物　　　　　　　　　　building

外国人登録証　　　　　alien registration card

~~~~~~~~~~~~~~~~~~~~~~~~~~~~~~

聖徳太子　　　　　　　Prince Shotoku (574－622)

法隆寺　　　　　　　　Horyuji Temple, a temple in Nara Prefecture built by Prince Shotoku at the beginning of the 7th century

元気茶　　　　　　　　fictitious tea

本田駅　　　　　　　　fictitious station

図書館前　　　　　　　fictitious bus stop

II. Translation

Sentence Patterns

1. When you borrow books from the library, you need a card.
2. Push this button, and change will come out.

Example Sentences

1. Do you often watch TV?
   ···Well, I watch it when there is a baseball game on.
2. What do you do when there is nothing in the refrigerator?
   ···I go out and eat something at a nearby restaurant.
3. Did you turn off the air conditioner when you left the meeting room?
   ···I am sorry, I forgot.
4. Where do you buy your clothes and shoes, Mr. Santos?
   ···I buy them in my country when I go back on summer vacation or New Year vacation.
   Because the things in Japan are small for me.
5. What is that?
   ···It's "Genki-cha." I take this when I'm not in good shape.
6. Won't you come to my house when you are free?
   ···Thank you. I would love to.
7. Did you work part-time when you were a student?
   ···Yes. I sometimes did.
8. The volume is low, isn't it?
   ···Turn this knob to the right, and the volume will go up.
9. Excuse me. Where is the City Hall?
   ···Go straight down this road, and you will find it on your left.

Conversation

How can I get there?

Librarian:	Hello. This is Midori Library.
Karina:	Er, could you tell me how to get there?
Librarian:	Take a No.12 bus from Honda Station, and get off at Toshokan-mae. It's the third stop.
Karina:	The third stop, right?
Librarian:	Yes. When you get off the bus, you will see a park in front of you. Our library is the white building in the park.
Karina:	I see. Is anything required when I borrow books?
Librarian:	Are you a foreigner?
Karina:	Yes, I am.
Librarian:	Then, please bring your alien registration card.
Karina:	Yes, I will. Thank you very much.

III. Reference Words & Information

道路・交通　ROAD & TRAFFIC

① 歩道　　　　sidewalk, pavement
② 車道　　　　road
③ 高速道路　　expressway, motorway
④ 通り　　　　street
⑤ 交差点　　　crossing
⑥ 横断歩道　　pedestrian crossing
⑦ 歩道橋　　　pedestrian bridge
⑧ 角　　　　　corner

⑨ 信号　　　　traffic light
⑩ 坂　　　　　slope
⑪ 踏切　　　　railroad crossing
⑫ ガソリンスタンド　gas station

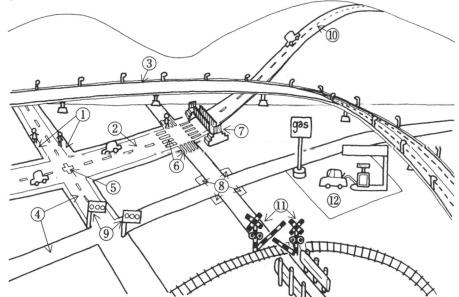

止まれ
stop

進入禁止
no entry

一方通行
one way

駐車禁止
no parking

右折禁止
no turning right

IV. Grammar Explanation

1.
V dictionary form V ない-form い-adj (〜い) な-adjな Nの	} とき、〜	When..., ...

とき connects two sentences and expresses the time when the state or action described in the main sentence exists or occurs. As shown in the table above, the forms of verbs, い-adjectives, な-adjectives and nouns connected to とき are the same as the forms when modifying nouns.

① 図書館で 本を 借りる とき、カードが 要ります。

    When you borrow books from the library, you need a card.

② 使い方が わからない とき、わたしに 聞いて ください。

    When you don't know how to use it, ask me.

③ 体の 調子が 悪い とき、「元気茶」を 飲みます。

    When I'm not in good shape, I drink "Genki-cha."

④ 暇な とき、うちへ 遊びに 来ませんか。

    Won't you come to my place when you are free?

⑤ 妻が 病気の とき、会社を 休みます。

    When my wife is sick, I take a day off work.

⑥ 若い とき、あまり 勉強しませんでした。

    When I was young, I did not study much.

⑦ 子どもの とき、よく 川で 泳ぎました。

    I used to swim in a river when I was a child.

The tense of adjective sentences and noun sentences which modify とき is not affected by the tense of the main sentence (see ⑥ and ⑦).

2.
V dictionary form V た-form	} とき、〜

When the dictionary form of the predicate is put before とき it indicates the non-completion of the action, and when the た-form of the predicate is put before とき it indicates the completion of the action.

⑧ 国へ 帰る とき、かばんを 買いました。

    I bought a bag when I went back to my country.

⑨ 国へ 帰った とき、かばんを 買いました。

    I bought a bag when I went back to my country.

In ⑧, かえる indicates that at the time being referred to the action had not been completed, that the speaker had not reached his/her country yet and that he/she bought a bag somewhere on his/her way there (Japan is included). In ⑨, かえった indicates that the action was completed and the speaker bought a bag after arriving in his/her country.

3. | V dictionary form と、〜 | ..., then (inevitably)...

When expressing the situation where, as a result of a certain action, another action or matter inevitably happens, と is used to connect the sentences.

⑩ この ボタンを 押すと、お釣りが 出ます。

    Press this button, and the change will come out.

⑪ これを 回すと、音が 大きく なります。

    Turn this, and the volume will go up.

⑫ 右へ 曲がると、郵便局が あります。

    Turn to the right, and you will find the post office.

Expressions of one's will, hope, invitation or request cannot be used in the sentence which follows 〜と.

$$\times 時間が\ あると、\begin{cases} 映画を\ 見に\ 行きます。 & \text{(will)} \\ 映画を\ 見に\ 行きたいです。 & \text{(hope)} \\ 映画を\ 見に\ 行きませんか。 & \text{(invitation)} \\ ちょっと\ 手伝って\ ください。 & \text{(request)} \end{cases}$$

In those cases, the conditional expression 〜たら is used instead of 〜と (see Lesson 25).

4. | Nが adjective ／ V |

You learned in Lesson 14 that the subject is indicated by が when describing a natural phenomenon. When describing a state or a scene as it is, the subject is also indicated by が.

⑬ 音が 小さいです。

    The volume is low.

⑭ 電気が 明るく なりました。

    The light became brighter.

⑮ この ボタンを 押すと、切符が 出ます。

    Press this button, and a ticket will come out.

5. | N (place) を V (verb of movement) |

The particle を is used to denote the place where a person or a thing passes. The verb of movement such as さんぽします, わたります, あるきます, etc. are used in this pattern.

⑯ 公園を 散歩します。   I take a walk in the park. (L. 13)

⑰ 道を 渡ります。   I cross the road.

⑱ 交差点を 右へ 曲がります。   I turn to the right at the intersection.

Lesson 24

I. Vocabulary

くれます Ⅱ		give (me)
つれて いきます Ⅰ	連れて 行きます	take (someone)
つれて きます Ⅲ	連れて 来ます	bring (someone)
おくります Ⅰ 　[ひとを ～]	送ります 　[人を ～]	escort [someone], go with
しょうかいします Ⅲ	紹介します	introduce
あんないします Ⅲ	案内します	show around, show the way
せつめいします Ⅲ	説明します	explain
いれます Ⅱ 　[コーヒーを ～]		make [coffee]
おじいさん／おじいちゃん		grandfather, old man
おばあさん／おばあちゃん		grandmother, old woman
じゅんび	準備	preparation (～します: prepare)
いみ	意味	meaning
［お］かし	［お］菓子	sweets, snacks
ぜんぶ	全部	all
じぶんで	自分で	by oneself

<◀会話▶

ほかに   besides
ワゴン車   station wagon
［お］弁当   box lunch

～～～～～～～～～～～～～～～～～

母の　日   Mother's Day

II. Translation

Sentence Patterns

1. Ms. Sato gave me a Christmas card.
2. I lent Ms. Kimura a book.
3. I was told the telephone number of the hospital by Mr. Yamada.
4. My mother sent me a sweater.

Example Sentences

1. Do you like your grandmother, Taro?
   ···Yes, I do. She always gives me some sweets.

2. This is very delicious wine.
   ···Yes. Ms. Sato gave it to me. It's French wine.

3. Taro, what will you do for your mother on Mother's Day?
   ···I will play the piano for her.

4. Mr. Miller, did you cook all the dishes for the party yesterday by yourself?
   ···No, Mr. Wang helped me.

5. Did you go by train?
   ···No, Mr. Yamada drove me.

Conversation

Will you help me?

Karina:	Mr. Wang, you are moving house tomorrow, aren't you? Shall I come to help you?
Wang:	Thank you. Well, then, will you come around 9 o'clock?
Karina:	Who else will come to help you?
Wang:	Mr. Yamada and Mr. Miller are coming.
Karina:	What about a car?
Wang:	Mr. Yamada will lend me his station wagon.
Karina:	What about lunch?
Wang:	Well....
Karina:	Shall I bring lunch?
Wang:	Thank you. Please.
Karina:	Then see you tomorrow.

III. Reference Words & Information

贈答の習慣 EXCHANGE OF PRESENTS

お年玉 — small gift of money given by parents and relatives to children on New Year's Day

入学祝い — gift celebrating admission to schools

卒業祝い — graduation gift (money, stationery, book, etc.)

結婚祝い — wedding gift (money, household goods, etc.)

出産祝い — gift celebrating a birth (baby clothes, toys, etc.)

お中元 [Jul. or Aug.]
お歳暮 [Dec.] — gift for a person whose care you are under, e.g., doctor, teacher, boss, etc. (food, etc.)

お香典 — condolence money

お見舞い — present given when visiting a sick person (flowers, fruits, etc.)

 熨斗袋 Special Envelope for Gift of Money
There are several kinds of special envelopes called NOSHIBUKURO. According to the occasion, a suitable one should be chosen.

for weddings
(with red and white, or gold and silver ribbon)

for celebrations other than weddings
(with red and white, or gold and silver ribbon)

for funerals
(with black and white ribbon)

IV. Grammar Explanation

1. くれます

You learned that あげます means "give" in Lesson 7. This verb cannot be used when somebody else gives something to the speaker or the speaker's family, etc. (×さとうさんは わたしに クリスマスカードを あげました). In this case くれます is used.

① わたしは 佐藤さんに 花を あげました。

I gave flowers to Ms. Sato.

② 佐藤さんは わたしに クリスマスカードを くれました。

Ms. Sato gave me a Christmas card.

③ 佐藤さんは 妹に お菓子を くれました。

Ms. Sato gave candies to my younger sister.

2.

V て-form	あげます もらいます くれます

あげます, もらいます and くれます are also used to refer to the giving and receiving of actions as well as those of things. They indicate who is doing that act for whom, while also expressing a sense of goodwill or gratitude. In this case, the act is expressed by the て-form.

1) V て-form あげます

V て-form あげます indicates that one does something for somebody with a sense of goodwill.

④ わたしは 木村さんに 本を 貸して あげました。

I lent Ms. Kimura a book.

When the speaker is the actor and the listener is the receiver of the act, this expression could give the impression that the speaker is being patronizing. You are, therefore, advised to avoid using this expression directly to someone whom you do not know very well or who is senior or superior to you. You may use it to someone with whom you have a very close, friendly relationship. So, when you offer assistance to someone who is not very close, V ます-form ましょうか (see Lesson 14, 6) is used.

⑤ タクシーを 呼びましょうか。   Shall I call a taxi for you?   (L. 14)

⑥ 手伝いましょうか。   May I help you?   (L. 14)

2) **Vて-form もらいます**

⑦ わたしは 山田さんに 図書館の 電話番号を 教えて もらいました。

    Mr. Yamada told me the telephone number of the library.

This expression conveys a sense of gratitude on the part of those who   receive a favor.

3) **Vて-form くれます**

⑧ 母は [わたしに] セーターを 送って くれました。

    My mother sent me a sweater.

Like Vて-form もらいます, this expression also conveys a sense of gratitude on the part of those who receive a favor. The difference is that Vて-form もらいます has the receiver of the act as the subject of the sentence, while Vて-form くれます has the actor as the subject of the sentence, implying the actor (the subject) voluntarily takes the action. The receiver of the act in the latter case is often the speaker and わたし(the receiver)に is often omitted.

3. **N (person) が V**

⑨ すてきな ネクタイですね。   That's a nice tie, isn't it?

  …ええ、佐藤さんが くれました。   …Yes. Ms. Sato gave it to me.

You present a topic, saying すてきな ネクタイですね. Responding to it, your partner in conversation gives a piece of information on the topic which is unknown to you, [この ネクタイは] さとうさんが くれました. The subject of the sentence giving new information is indicated by が.

4. **Interrogative が V**

You learned that when the subject is questioned, it is indicated by が in あります／います sentences (Lesson 10) and adjective sentences (Lesson 12). This is also the case for verb sentences.

⑩ だれが 手伝いに 行きますか。   Who will go to give him a hand?

  …カリナさんが 行きます。   …Ms. Karina will.

Lesson 25

I. Vocabulary

かんがえます II	考えます	think, consider
つきます I	着きます	arrive [at the station]
［えきに～］	［駅に～］	
りゅうがくします III	留学します	study abroad
とります I	取ります	grow old
［としを～］	［年を～］	
いなか	田舎	countryside, hometown
たいしかん	大使館	embassy
グループ		group
チャンス		chance
おく	億	hundred million
もし ［～たら］		if ～
いくら ［～ても］		however ～, even if ～

◁◀会話▶▷

転勤 <small>てんきん</small>	transfer (〜します: be transferred to another office)
こと	thing, matter (〜の こと: thing about 〜)
一杯 飲みましょう。 <small>いっぱい のみ</small>	Let's have a drink together.
［いろいろ］お世話に なりました。 <small>せわ</small>	Thank you for everything you have done for me.
頑張ります Ⅰ <small>がんば</small>	do one's best
どうぞ お元気で。 <small>げんき</small>	Best of luck. (said when expecting a long separation)

II. Translation

Sentence Patterns

1. If it rains, I will not go out.
2. Even if it rains, I will go out.

Example Sentences

1. If you had a hundred million yen, what would you like to do?
   ···I would want to build a computer software company.
2. What will you do if your friend doesn't come at the time he promised?
   ···I will go home immediately.
3. That new shoe shop has a lot of good shoes.
   ···Does it? If their prices are reasonable, I would like to buy some.
4. Do I have to submit the report by tomorrow?
   ···No. If it's not possible, submit it on Friday.
5. Have you thought of a name for your baby yet?
   ···Yes. If it is a boy, he will be named "Hikaru," and if it is a girl, she
   will be named "Aya."
6. Will you start work straightaway after you graduate from university?
   ···No, I want to travel to various countries for about one year.
7. Excuse me, ma'am. But I don't understand the meaning of this word.
   ···Did you check it in the dictionary?
   Yes, I did. I still don't get it.
8. Japanese people are fond of traveling in groups, aren't they?
   ···Yes, they are, because it is economical.
   No matter how economical it is, I don't like group tours.

Conversation

Thank you for having been kind to me

Yamada:	Congratulations! You are going to be transferred.
Miller:	Thank you.
Kimura:	When you leave for Tokyo, we will miss you.
	Don't forget about Osaka after you go to Tokyo.
Miller:	Of course. Ms. Kimura, if you have time, please come to Tokyo.
Santos:	Mr. Miller, when you come to Osaka, give me a call.
	Let's have a drink.
Miller:	I'd love to.
	Thank you very much, all of you, for having been kind to me.
Sato:	Please take care of yourself and do your best.
Miller:	Yes, I will do my best. Best of luck, all of you.

IIII. Reference Words & Information

人の一生　LIFE

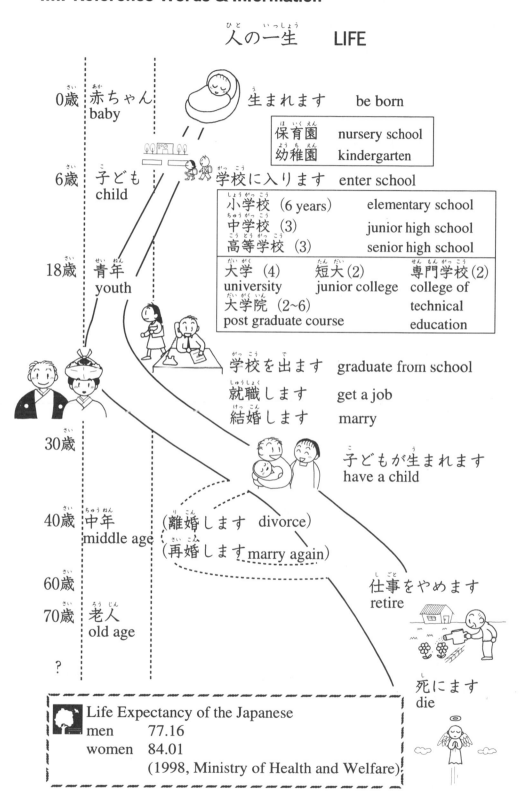

0歳　赤ちゃん　baby

生まれます　be born

保育園	nursery school
幼稚園	kindergarten

6歳　子ども　child

学校に入ります　enter school

小学校（6 years）	elementary school
中学校（3）	junior high school
高等学校（3）	senior high school
大学（4）　短大（2）　専門学校（2）	
university　junior college　college of	
大学院（2〜6）	technical
post graduate course	education

18歳　青年　youth

学校を出ます　graduate from school

就職します　get a job

結婚します　marry

子どもが生まれます
have a child

30歳

40歳　中年　middle age

（離婚します　divorce）

（再婚します　marry again）

60歳

70歳　老人　old age

?

仕事をやめます
retire

死にます
die

Life Expectancy of the Japanese
men　　77.16
women　84.01
　　　（1998, Ministry of Health and Welfare）

IV. Grammar Explanation

1. | plain past form ら、 〜 | If...

When ら is attached to the past tense plain form of verbs, adjectives, etc., it changes the preceding clause into a conditional expression. When a speaker wants to state his opinion, situation, request, etc., in the conditional, this pattern is used.

① お金が あったら、旅行します。

　　If I had money, I would travel.

② 時間が なかったら、テレビを 見ません。

　　If I don't have time, I will not watch TV.

③ 安かったら、パソコンを 買いたいです。

　　If it's inexpensive, I want to buy a personal computer.

④ 暇だったら、手伝って ください。

　　If you are free, please give me a hand.

⑤ いい 天気だったら、散歩しませんか。

　　If it's fine, won't you take a walk with me?

2. | V た-form ら、 〜 | When... ／ After...

This pattern is used to express that a certain action will be done or a certain situation will appear when a matter, action or state which is sure to happen in the future has been completed or achieved. The main sentence is always in the present tense.

⑥ 10時に なったら、出かけましょう。

　　Let's go out when it gets to ten.

⑦ うちへ 帰ったら、すぐ シャワーを 浴びます。

　　I take a shower soon after I return home.

3. | V て-form
い-adj (〜い)→〜くて
な-adj [な] →で
N で } も、 〜 | Even if...

This expression is used to present a reverse condition. Contrary to plain past form ら、 〜, this expression is used when an action which is expected to be taken or an event which is expected to happen naturally under the given circumstances does not materialize or a thing turns out in a way opposite to a socially accepted idea.

⑧ 雨が 降っても、洗濯します。

Even if it rains, I'll do the laundry.

⑨ 安くても、わたしは グループ旅行が 嫌いです。

Even if group tours are inexpensive, I don't like them.

⑩ 便利でも、パソコンを 使いません。

Even if a personal computer is useful, I won't use it.

⑪ 日曜日でも、働きます。

Even if it is Sunday, I will work.

4. もし and いくら

もし is used in a sentence in the plain past form to indicate beforehand that the sentence is going to present a condition, while いくら is used with ～ても(～でも) to do the same. もし implies that an emphasis is on the speaker's supposition while いくら is meant to stress the degree of conditionality.

⑫ もし 1億円 あったら、いろいろな 国を 旅行したいです。

If I had 100 million yen, I would want to travel in various countries.

⑬ いくら 考えても、わかりません。

No matter how much I think, I can't understand this.

⑭ いくら 高くても、買います。

No matter how expensive it is, I will buy it.

5. Nが

As mentioned in Lesson 16, 4. [Note], the subject of a subordinate clause is indicated by が. In subordinate clauses using たら、ても、とき、と、まえに、etc., in addition to から, the subject is indicated by が, as shown below.

⑮ 友達が 来る まえに、部屋を 掃除します。

I will clean my room before my friends come.　　　　　　　　　　(L. 18)

⑯ 妻が 病気の とき、会社を 休みます。

When my wife is sick, I take a day off work.　　　　　　　　　　(L. 23)

⑰ 友達が 約束の 時間に 来なかったら、どう しますか。

If your friend doesn't come on time, what will you do?　　　　　(L. 25)

SUMMARY LESSON

I. Particles

1. ［は］

  A: 1) I am Mike Miller.   (Lesson 1)

      2) I get up at six in the morning.   (4)

      3) Cherry blossoms are beautiful.   (8)

  B: 1) What time is it now in New York?   (4)

      2) On Sunday I went to Nara with a friend.   (6)

      3) Tokyo Disneyland is in Chiba Prefecture.   (10)

      4) Please send the data by fax.   (17)

2. ［も］

  A: 1) Maria is Brazilian, too.   (1)

      2) Please send this parcel, too.   (11)

      3) I like both.   (12)

      4) I have been on a diet many times.   (19)

  B: 1) I did not go anywhere.   (5)

      2) I did not eat anything.   (6)

      3) There was no one.   (10)

3. ［の］

  A: 1) That person is Mr. Miller of IMC.   (1)

      2) This is a book on computers.   (2)

      3) That is my umbrella.   (2)

      4) This is a Japanese car.   (3)

      5) Did you study last night?   (4)

      6) How are your Japanese studies going?   (8)

      7) There is a picture on the desk.   (10)

      8) Please tell me how to read this Kanji.   (14)

      9) I came from Bandung, Indonesia.   (16)

  B: 1) This bag is Ms. Sato's.   (2)

      2) Where was this camera made?

         ···In Japan.   (3)

  C: Is there one a little bigger?   (14)

4. ［を］

  A: 1) I drink juice.   (6)

      2) I am going to travel for a week.   (11)

      3) I will pick up my child at two o'clock. (13)

163

B: 1) I took a day off work yesterday. (11)
    2) I leave home at eight every morning. (13)
    3) I get off the train at Kyoto. (16)
C: 1) I take a walk in a park every morning. (13)
    2) Please cross at that traffic signal. (23)
    3) Go straight along this street and you will find the station. (23)

5. [が]

A: 1) I like Italian food. (9)
    2) Mr. Miller is good at cooking. (9)
    3) I understand Japanese a little. (9)
    4) Do you have any small change? (9)
    5) I have two children. (11)
    6) I want a personal computer. (13)
    7) Can you ski? (18)
    8) I need a tape recorder. (20)
B: 1) There is a man over there. (10)
    2) There is a picture on the desk. (10)
    3) There will be a festival in Kyoto next month. (21)
C: 1) Tokyo has a big population. (12)
    2) Mr. Santos is tall. (16)
    3) I have a sore throat. (17)
D: 1) Which is faster, a bus or a train?
      ···A train is faster. (12)
    2) Baseball is the most interesting of all the sports. (12)
E: 1) It is raining now. (14)
    2) Touch this, and the water will come out. (23)
    3) The volume is low. (23)
F: 1) I am going to go and have a meal after the concert is over. (16)
    2) What will you do if your friend does not come on time? (25)
    3) When my wife is sick, I take a day off work. (23)
    4) Which is the picture that Ms. Karina drew? (22)
G: 1) Ms. Sato gave me wine. (24)
    2) Who paid for you? (24)

6. [に]

A: 1) I get up at six o'clock in the morning. (4)
    2) I came to Japan on March 25th. (5)
B: 1) I gave some flowers to Ms. Kimura. (7)
    2) I write Christmas cards to my family and friends. (7)

C: 1) I received a gift from Mr. Santos. (7)
   2) I borrowed a book from a person in the company. (7)
D: 1) There is a picture on the desk. (10)
   2) My family is in New York. (10)
   3) Maria lives in Osaka. (15)
E: 1) I will meet a friend tomorrow. (6)
   2) Have you already got accustomed to living in Japan? (8)
   3) Let's go in that coffee shop. (13)
   4) Please sit here. (15)
   5) I take a train from Umeda. (16)
   6) Please write your name here. (14)
   7) Touch this, and the water will come out. (23)
F: I play tennis once a week. (11)
G: 1) I came to Japan to study economics. (13)
   2) I will go to Kyoto for cherry blossom viewing. (13)
H: Teresa became ten. (19)

7. [へ]

   1) I will go to Kyoto with a friend. (5)
   2) I will go to France to study cooking. (13)
   3) Please turn right at that traffic light. (14)

8. [で]

A: 1) I go home by taxi. (5)
   2) I send the data by fax. (7)
   3) Do you write reports in Japanese? (7)
B: 1) I buy a newspaper at the station. (6)
   2) In July there is a festival in Kyoto. (21)
C: I like summer the best of the year. (12)

9. [と]

A: 1) I came to Japan with my family. (5)
   2) Ms. Sato is talking with the department chief in the meeting room. (14)
B: 1) I have Saturdays and Sundays off. (4)
   2) The book store is between a florist's and a supermarket. (10)
   3) Which is more interesting, football or baseball? (12)
C: 1) I think it will rain tomorrow. (21)
   2) The prime minister said that he would go to America next month. (21)

10. [や]

   There are old letters, pictures and things in the box. (10)

11. [から] [まで]

  A: 1) I work from nine to five.   (4)
       2) The bank is open from nine to three.   (4)
       3) I worked until ten last night.   (4)
  B: 1) Chili sauce is on the second rack from the bottom.   (10)
       2) It takes four hours to fly from my country to Japan.   (11)
       3) Shall I come and get you at the station?   (14)

12. [までに]

    I have to return the books by Saturday.   (17)

13. [より]

    China is bigger than Japan.   (12)

14. [でも]

    Shall we drink a glass of beer or something?   (21)

15. [か]

  A: 1) Is Mr. Santos Brazilian?   (1)
       2) Is it a mechanical pencil or a ballpoint pen?   (2)
       3) Shall we go and see a film together?   (6)
  B: Excuse me. Where is Yunyu-ya store?
         ···Yunyu-ya store? It's in that building.   (10)
  C: Is this umbrella yours?
         ···No, it isn't. It's Mr. Schmidt's.
         I see.   (2)

16. [ね]

    1) I studied until twelve last night, too.
       ···That's tough, isn't it?   (4)
    2) That spoon looks nice, doesn't it?   (7)
    3) Well,···let me see, it's 871-6813.
       ···871-6813, right?   (4)
    4) You see the man over there. Who is he?   (10)

17. [よ]

    Does this train go to Koshien?
    ···No. The next local train does.   (5)

II. How to Use the Forms

1. [ます-form]
ます-formませんか	Won't you have some tea with me?	(Lesson 6)
ます-formましょう	Let's meet at five.	(6)
ます-formたいです	I want to buy a camera.	(13)
ます-formに いきます	I go to see a movie.	(13)
ます-formましょうか	Shall I call a taxi for you?	(14)

2. [て-form]
て-form ください	Please lend me your ballpoint pen.	(14)
て-form います	Ms. Sato is now talking with Mr. Miller.	(14)
	Maria lives in Osaka.	(15)
て-formも いいです	May I smoke?	(15)
て-formは いけません	Don't take photographs in the museum.	(15)
て-formから、～	After I finish work, I go swimming.	(16)
て-form、て-form、～	In the morning, I go jogging, take a shower, then go to the office.	(16)
て-form あげます	I lend a CD to Mr. Miller.	(24)
て-form もらいます	Ms. Sato took me to Osaka Castle.	(24)
て-form くれます	Mr. Yamada took me in his car.	(24)

3. [ない-form]
ない-formないで ください	Please do not take photographs here.	(17)
ない-formなければ なりません	You must show your passport.	(17)
ない-formなくても いいです	You don't need to take off your shoes.	(17)

4. [dictionary form]
dictionary form ことができます	I can play the piano.	(18)
dictionary form ことです	My hobby is watching movies.	(18)
dictionary form まえに、～	I read a book before going to bed.	(18)
dictionary formと、～	Turn to the right, and you'll find a post office.	(23)

5. [た-form]
た-form ことが あります	I have been to Hokkaido.	(19)
た-formり、た-formり します	On my holidays I play tennis, take walks and so forth.	(19)

167

6. **[plain form]**

plain formと おもいます	I think that Mr. Miller has already gone home.(21)
	I think that things are expensive in Japan. (21)
	I think that family is the most important thing. (21)
plain formと いいます	My brother said that he would return by ten. (21)

verb }
い-adjective } **plain form**
な-adjective | **plain form** } でしょう？
noun } ～だ

Tomorrow you will go to the party, won't you?(21)
The morning rush hours are terrible, aren't they?(21)
Personal computers are useful, aren't they? (21)
He is American, isn't he? (21)

verb plain form noun	This is the cake that I made. (22)

7. **verb plain form**
い-adjective
な-adjective な } とき、～
noun の

When I read a paper, I put on my glasses. (23)
When I am sleepy, I drink coffee. (23)
When I have time, I watch video tapes. (23)
When it rains, I take a taxi. (23)

8. **plain form past** ら、～

If I have a personal computer, it'll be convenient. (25)
If the personal computer is cheap, I will buy it. (25)
If it's simple to use, I will buy it. (25)
If it's fine, I'll take a walk. (25)

9. **verb て-form**

い-adjective ～くて } も、～

な-adjective で
noun で

Though I've checked in the dictionary, I don't understand its meaning. (25)
Even if personal computers are cheap, I won't buy one. (25)
Even if you don't like it, you should eat it. (25)
He works even on Sundays. (25)

III. Adverbs and Adverbial Expressions

1. みんな　　　The foreign teachers are all Americans.　　　(Lesson 11)
　　ぜんぶ　　　I have finished all my homework.　　　(24)
　　たくさん　　I have a lot of work.　　　(9)
　　とても　　　It is very cold in Beijing.　　　(8)
　　よく　　　　Mr. Wang understands English well.　　　(9)
　　だいたい　　Teresa understands most Hiragana.　　　(9)
　　すこし　　　Maria understands Katakana a little.　　　(9)
　　ちょっと　　Let's take a rest for a while.　　　(6)
　　もう すこし　Don't you have one a little bit smaller?　　　(14)
　　もう　　　　Make one more copy, please.　　　(14)
　　ずっと　　　There are a lot more people in Tokyo than in New York.　(12)
　　いちばん　　I like tempura best of all Japanese dishes.　　　(12)
　　　　　　　　Notebooks are on the top of that shelf.　　　(10)

2. いつも　　　I always have lunch in the university dining hall.　　(6)
　　ときどき　　I sometimes eat at a restaurant.　　　(6)
　　よく　　　　Mr. Miller often goes to coffee shops.　　　(22)
　　はじめて　　Yesterday I ate sushi for the first time.　　　(12)
　　また　　　　Please come again tomorrow.　　　(14)
　　もう いちど　Once again, please.　　　(II)

3. いま　　　　It is now ten past two.　　　(4)
　　すぐ　　　　Please send the report at once.　　　(14)
　　もう　　　　I have already bought my Shinkansen ticket.　　　(7)
　　　　　　　　It's eight o'clock now, isn't it?　　　(8)
　　まだ　　　　Have you had lunch?
　　　　　　　　…No, not yet.　　　(7)
　　これから　　I'm going to take lunch from now.　　　(7)
　　そろそろ　　It is almost time for me to leave.　　　(8)
　　あとで　　　I will come later.　　　(14)
　　まず　　　　First, push this button.　　　(16)
　　つぎに　　　Next, insert the card.　　　(16)
　　さいきん　　Recently Japanese football teams have become stronger.　(21)

4. じぶんで　　I cooked all the dishes for the party by myself.　　(24)
　　ひとりで　　I go to the hospital alone.　　　(5)
　　みんなで　　We will go to Kyoto all together tomorrow.　　　(20)
　　いっしょに　Won't you drink some beer with me?　　　(6)
　　べつべつに　Please charge us separately.　　　(13)
　　ぜんぶで　　It is five hundred yen in all.　　　(11)

ほかに	Who will come to help you other than me?	(24)
はやく	I'll go home early.	(9)
ゆっくり	Please speak slowly.	(14)
	Have a good rest, today.	(17)
だんだん	It will get hotter and hotter from now on.	(19)
まっすぐ	Please go straight.	(14)

5.
あまり	That dictionary is not very good.	(8)
ぜんぜん	I don't understand Indonesian at all.	(9)
なかなか	You can hardly ever see horses in Japan.	(18)
いちども	I have never eaten sushi.	(19)
ぜひ	I am eager to go to Hokkaido.	(18)
たぶん	I think Mr. Miller probably doesn't know.	(21)
きっと	I am sure it will be fine tomorrow.	(21)
もし	If I had one hundred million yen, I would like to form my own company.	(25)
いくら	However cheap group tours are, I don't like them.	(25)

6.
とくに	In that film, the father, especially, acted well.	(15)
じつは	I am on a diet actually.	(19)
ほんとうに	I think food really costs a lot in Japan.	(21)
もちろん	I think Brazil will win the game, of course.	(21)

IV. Various Conjunctions

1. そして　　　Subways in Tokyo are clean and convenient.　　　(Lesson 8)
　　〜で　　　　Nara is a quiet and beautiful city.　　　(16)
　　〜くて　　　This personal computer is light and handy.　　　(16)
　　それから　　Send this by special delivery, please. And this parcel, too.　(11)
　　〜たり　　　On holidays I play tennis, go on walks and so on.　　　(19)
　　〜が　　　　Excuse me, but lend me a ballpoint pen, please.　　　(14)

2. それから　　I studied Japanese, and then saw a movie.　　　(6)
　　〜てから　　We dined at a restaurant after the concert was over.　　　(16)
　　〜て、〜て　In the morning I jog, take a shower, and go to the office.　　(16)
　　〜まえに　　I write in my diary before going to bed.　　　(18)
　　〜とき　　　When you borrow books from the library, you need a card.　(23)

3. から　　　　I don't go anywhere, because I don't have the time.　　　(9)
　　ですから　　Today is my wife's birthday. So I must go home early.　　(17)

4. 〜が　　　　'The Seven Samurai' is an old but interesting movie.　　　(8)
　　でも　　　　The tour was fun. But I got tired.　　　(12)
　　〜けど　　　This curry is hot but tasty.　　　(20)
　　しかし　　　Dancing is good for the health, so I will practice it every
　　　　　　　　day from tomorrow.
　　　　　　　　…But excessive practice is not good for one's health.　　(19)

5. じゃ　　　　This is an Italian wine.
　　　　　　　　…Well, I'll buy it.　　　(3)
　　〜と　　　　Push this button, and change will come out.　　　(23)
　　〜たら　　　If it rains, I will not go out.　　　(25)

6. 〜ても　　　Even if it rains, I will go out.　　　(25)

171

APPENDICES

I. Numerals

0	ゼロ、れい	100	ひゃく
1	いち	200	にひゃく
2	に	300	さんびゃく
3	さん	400	よんひゃく
4	よん、し	500	ごひゃく
5	ご	600	ろっぴゃく
6	ろく	700	ななひゃく
7	なな、しち	800	はっぴゃく
8	はち	900	きゅうひゃく
9	きゅう、く		
10	じゅう	1,000	せん
11	じゅういち	2,000	にせん
12	じゅうに	3,000	さんぜん
13	じゅうさん	4,000	よんせん
14	じゅうよん、じゅうし	5,000	ごせん
15	じゅうご	6,000	ろくせん
16	じゅうろく	7,000	ななせん
17	じゅうなな、じゅうしち	8,000	はっせん
18	じゅうはち	9,000	きゅうせん
19	じゅうきゅう、じゅうく		
20	にじゅう	10,000	いちまん
30	さんじゅう	100,000	じゅうまん
40	よんじゅう	1,000,000	ひゃくまん
50	ごじゅう	10,000,000	せんまん
60	ろくじゅう	100,000,000	いちおく
70	ななじゅう、しちじゅう		
80	はちじゅう	17.5	じゅうななてんご
90	きゅうじゅう	0.83	れいてんはちさん

$\frac{1}{2}$ にぶんの いち

$\frac{3}{4}$ よんぶんの さん

II. Expressions of time

day	morning	night
おととい the day before yesterday	おとといの あさ the morning before last	おとといの ばん the night before last
きのう yesterday	きのうの あさ yesterday morning	きのうの ばん last night
きょう today	けさ this morning	こんばん tonight
あした tomorrow	あしたの あさ tomorrow morning	あしたの ばん tomorrow night
あさって the day after tomorrow	あさっての あさ the morning after next	あさっての ばん the night after next
まいにち every day	まいあさ every morning	まいばん every night

week	month	year
せんせんしゅう （にしゅうかんまえ） the week before last	せんせんげつ （にかげつまえ） the month before last	おととし the year before last
せんしゅう last week	せんげつ last month	きょねん last year
こんしゅう this week	こんげつ this month	ことし this year
らいしゅう next week	らいげつ next month	らいねん next year
さらいしゅう the week after next	さらいげつ the month after next	さらいねん the year after next
まいしゅう every week	まいつき every month	まいとし、まいねん every year

Telling time

o'clock　一時		minute　一分	
1	いちじ	1	いっぷん
2	にじ	2	にふん
3	さんじ	3	さんぷん
4	よじ	4	よんぷん
5	ごじ	5	ごふん
6	ろくじ	6	ろっぷん
7	しちじ	7	ななふん、しちふん
8	はちじ	8	はっぷん
9	くじ	9	きゅうふん
10	じゅうじ	10	じゅっぷん、じっぷん
11	じゅういちじ	15	じゅうごふん
12	じゅうにじ	30	さんじゅっぷん、さんじっぷん、はん
?	なんじ	?	なんぷん

the days of the week
～曜日

にちようび	Sunday
げつようび	Monday
かようび	Tuesday
すいようび	Wednesday
もくようび	Thursday
きんようび	Friday
どようび	Saturday
なんようび	what day

174

date

month　一月		day　一日			
1	いちがつ	1	ついたち	17	じゅうしちにち
2	にがつ	2	ふつか	18	じゅうはちにち
3	さんがつ	3	みっか	19	じゅうくにち
4	しがつ	4	よっか	20	はつか
5	ごがつ	5	いつか	21	にじゅういちにち
6	ろくがつ	6	むいか	22	にじゅうににち
7	しちがつ	7	なのか	23	にじゅうさんにち
8	はちがつ	8	ようか	24	にじゅうよっか
9	くがつ	9	ここのか	25	にじゅうごにち
10	じゅうがつ	10	とおか	26	にじゅうろくにち
11	じゅういちがつ	11	じゅういちにち	27	にじゅうしちにち
12	じゅうにがつ	12	じゅうににち	28	にじゅうはちにち
?	なんがつ	13	じゅうさんにち	29	にじゅうくにち
		14	じゅうよっか	30	さんじゅうにち
		15	じゅうごにち	31	さんじゅういちにち
		16	じゅうろくにち	?	なんにち

III. Expressions of period

	time duration	
	hour －時間	minute －分
1	いちじかん	いっぷん
2	にじかん	にふん
3	さんじかん	さんぷん
4	よじかん	よんぷん
5	ごじかん	ごふん
6	ろくじかん	ろっぷん
7	ななじかん、しちじかん	ななふん、しちふん
8	はちじかん	はっぷん
9	くじかん	きゅうふん
10	じゅうじかん	じゅっぷん、じっぷん
?	なんじかん	なんぷん

	period			
	day －日	week －週間	month －か月	year －年
1	いちにち	いっしゅうかん	いっかげつ	いちねん
2	ふつか	にしゅうかん	にかげつ	にねん
3	みっか	さんしゅうかん	さんかげつ	さんねん
4	よっか	よんしゅうかん	よんかげつ	よねん
5	いつか	ごしゅうかん	ごかげつ	ごねん
6	むいか	ろくしゅうかん	ろっかげつ、はんとし	ろくねん
7	なのか	ななしゅうかん、しちしゅうかん	ななかげつ、しちかげつ	ななねん、しちねん
8	ようか	はっしゅうかん	はちかげつ、はっかげつ	はちねん
9	ここのか	きゅうしゅうかん	きゅうかげつ	きゅうねん
10	とおか	じゅっしゅうかん、じっしゅうかん	じゅっかげつ、じっかげつ	じゅうねん
?	なんにち	なんしゅうかん	なんかげつ	なんねん

IV. Counters

	things	persons	order	thin & flat things
		一人	一番	一枚
1	ひとつ	ひとり	いちばん	いちまい
2	ふたつ	ふたり	にばん	にまい
3	みっつ	さんにん	さんばん	さんまい
4	よっつ	よにん	よんばん	よんまい
5	いつつ	ごにん	ごばん	ごまい
6	むっつ	ろくにん	ろくばん	ろくまい
7	ななつ	ななにん、しちにん	ななばん	ななまい
8	やっつ	はちにん	はちばん	はちまい
9	ここのつ	きゅうにん	きゅうばん	きゅうまい
10	とお	じゅうにん	じゅうばん	じゅうまい
?	いくつ	なんにん	なんばん	なんまい

	machines & vehicles	age	books & notebooks	clothes
	一台	一歳	一冊	一着
1	いちだい	いっさい	いっさつ	いっちゃく
2	にだい	にさい	にさつ	にちゃく
3	さんだい	さんさい	さんさつ	さんちゃく
4	よんだい	よんさい	よんさつ	よんちゃく
5	ごだい	ごさい	ごさつ	ごちゃく
6	ろくだい	ろくさい	ろくさつ	ろくちゃく
7	ななだい	ななさい	ななさつ	ななちゃく
8	はちだい	はっさい	はっさつ	はっちゃく
9	きゅうだい	きゅうさい	きゅうさつ	きゅうちゃく
10	じゅうだい	じゅっさい、じっさい	じゅっさつ、じっさつ	じゅっちゃく、じっちゃく
?	なんだい	なんさい	なんさつ	なんちゃく

	frequency	small things	shoes & socks	houses
	一回	一個	一足	一軒
1	いっかい	いっこ	いっそく	いっけん
2	にかい	にこ	にそく	にけん
3	さんかい	さんこ	さんぞく	さんげん
4	よんかい	よんこ	よんそく	よんけん
5	ごかい	ごこ	ごそく	ごけん
6	ろっかい	ろっこ	ろくそく	ろっけん
7	ななかい	ななこ	ななそく	ななけん
8	はっかい	はっこ	はっそく	はっけん
9	きゅうかい	きゅうこ	きゅうそく	きゅうけん
10	じゅっかい、じっかい	じゅっこ、じっこ	じゅっそく、じっそく	じゅっけん、じっけん
?	なんかい	なんこ	なんぞく	なんげん

	floors of a building	thin & long things	drinks & so on in cups & glasses	small animals, fish & insects
	一階	一本	一杯	一匹
1	いっかい	いっぽん	いっぱい	いっぴき
2	にかい	にほん	にはい	にひき
3	さんがい	さんぼん	さんばい	さんびき
4	よんかい	よんほん	よんはい	よんひき
5	ごかい	ごほん	ごはい	ごひき
6	ろっかい	ろっぽん	ろっぱい	ろっぴき
7	ななかい	ななほん	ななはい	ななひき
8	はっかい	はっぽん	はっぱい	はっぴき
9	きゅうかい	きゅうほん	きゅうはい	きゅうひき
10	じゅっかい、じっかい	じゅっぽん、じっぽん	じゅっぱい、じっぱい	じゅっぴき、じっぴき
?	なんがい	なんぼん	なんばい	なんびき

V. Conjugation of verbs

I −group

	ます-form		て-form	dictionary form
会います [ともだちに ～]	あい	ます	あって	あう
遊びます	あそび	ます	あそんで	あそぶ
洗います	あらい	ます	あらって	あらう
あります	あり	ます	あって	ある
あります	あり	ます	あって	ある
あります [おまつりが ～]	あり	ます	あって	ある
歩きます [みちを ～]	あるき	ます	あるいて	あるく
言います	いい	ます	いって	いう
行きます	いき	ます	いって	いく
急ぎます	いそぎ	ます	いそいで	いそぐ
要ります [ビザが ～]	いり	ます	いって	いる
動きます [とけいが ～]	うごき	ます	うごいて	うごく
歌います	うたい	ます	うたって	うたう
売ります	うり	ます	うって	うる
置きます	おき	ます	おいて	おく
送ります	おくり	ます	おくって	おくる
送ります [ひとを ～]	おくり	ます	おくって	おくる
押します	おし	ます	おして	おす
思います	おもい	ます	おもって	おもう
思い出します	おもいだし	ます	おもいだして	おもいだす
泳ぎます	およぎ	ます	およいで	およぐ
終わります	おわり	ます	おわって	おわる
買います	かい	ます	かって	かう
返します	かえし	ます	かえして	かえす
帰ります	かえり	ます	かえって	かえる
かかります	かかり	ます	かかって	かかる
書きます	かき	ます	かいて	かく
貸します	かし	ます	かして	かす
勝ちます	かち	ます	かって	かつ
かぶります [ぼうしを ～]	かぶり	ます	かぶって	かぶる

ない-form		た-form	meaning	lesson
あわ	ない	あった	meet [a friend]	6
あそば	ない	あそんだ	enjoy oneself, play	13
あらわ	ない	あらった	wash	18
—	ない	あった	have	9
—	ない	あった	exist, be (inanimate things)	10
—	ない	あった	[a festival] be held, take place	21
あるか	ない	あるいた	walk [along a road]	23
いわ	ない	いった	say	21
いか	ない	いった	go	5
いそが	ない	いそいだ	hurry	14
いら	ない	いった	need, require [a visa]	20
うごか	ない	うごいた	[a watch] move, work	23
うたわ	ない	うたった	sing	18
うら	ない	うった	sell	15
おか	ない	おいた	put	15
おくら	ない	おくった	send	7
おくら	ない	おくった	escort [someone], go with	24
おさ	ない	おした	push, press	16
おもわ	ない	おもった	think	21
おもいださ	ない	おもいだした	remember, recollect	15
およが	ない	およいだ	swim	13
おわら	ない	おわった	finish	4
かわ	ない	かった	buy	6
かえさ	ない	かえした	give back, return	17
かえら	ない	かえった	go home, return	5
かから	ない	かかった	take (referring to time or money)	11
かか	ない	かいた	write, draw, paint	6
かさ	ない	かした	lend	7
かた	ない	かった	win	21
かぶら	ない	かぶった	put on [a hat, etc.]	22

	ます-form		て-form	dictionary form
聞きます	きき	ます	きいて	きく
聞きます [せんせいに 〜]	きき	ます	きいて	きく
切ります	きり	ます	きって	きる
消します	けし	ます	けして	けす
触ります [ドアに 〜]	さわり	ます	さわって	さわる
知ります	しり	ます	しって	しる
吸います [たばこを 〜]	すい	ます	すって	すう
住みます	すみ	ます	すんで	すむ
座ります	すわり	ます	すわって	すわる
立ちます	たち	ます	たって	たつ
出します [てがみを 〜]	だし	ます	だして	だす
出します	だし	ます	だして	だす
出します [レポートを 〜]	だし	ます	だして	だす
使います	つかい	ます	つかって	つかう
着きます [えきに 〜]	つき	ます	ついて	つく
作ります、造ります	つくり	ます	つくって	つくる
連れて 行きます	つれて いき	ます	つれて いって	つれて いく
手伝います	てつだい	ます	てつだって	てつだう
泊まります [ホテルに 〜]	とまり	ます	とまって	とまる
取ります	とり	ます	とって	とる
撮ります [しゃしんを 〜]	とり	ます	とって	とる
取ります [としを 〜]	とり	ます	とって	とる
直します	なおし	ます	なおして	なおす
なくします	なくし	ます	なくして	なくす
習います	ならい	ます	ならって	ならう
なります	なり	ます	なって	なる
脱ぎます	ぬぎ	ます	ぬいで	ぬぐ
登ります [やまに 〜]	のぼり	ます	のぼって	のぼる
飲みます	のみ	ます	のんで	のむ
飲みます [くすりを 〜]	のみ	ます	のんで	のむ

ない-form		た-form	meaning	lesson
きか	ない	きいた	hear, listen	6
きか	ない	きいた	ask [a teacher]	23
きら	ない	きった	cut, slice	7
けさ	ない	けした	turn off	14
さわら	ない	さわった	touch [a door]	23
しら	ない	しった	get to know	15
すわ	ない	すった	smoke [a cigarette]	6
すま	ない	すんだ	be going to live	15
すわら	ない	すわった	sit down	15
たた	ない	たった	stand up	15
ださ	ない	だした	send [a letter]	13
ださ	ない	だした	take out, withdraw	16
ださ	ない	だした	hand in [a report]	17
つかわ	ない	つかった	use	15
つか	ない	ついた	arrive [at the station]	25
つくら	ない	つくった	make, produce	15
つれていか	ない	つれていった	take (someone)	24
てつだわ	ない	てつだった	help (with a task)	14
とまら	ない	とよった	stay [at a hotel]	19
とら	ない	とった	take, pass	14
とら	ない	とった	take [a photograph]	6
とら	ない	とった	grow old	25
なおさ	ない	なおした	repair, correct	20
なくさ	ない	なくした	lose	17
ならわ	ない	ならった	learn	7
なら	ない	なった	become	19
ぬが	ない	ぬいだ	take off (clothes, shoes, etc.)	17
のぼら	ない	のぼった	climb [a mountain]	19
のま	ない	のんだ	drink	6
のま	ない	のんだ	take [medicine]	17

	ます-form		て-form	dictionary form
乗ります [でんしゃに～]	のり	ます	のって	のる
入ります [きっさてんに～]	はいり	ます	はいって	はいる
入ります [だいがくに～]	はいり	ます	はいって	はいる
入ります [おふろに～]	はいり	ます	はいって	はいる
はきます [くつを～]	はき	ます	はいて	はく
働きます	はたらき	ます	はたらいて	はたらく
弾きます	ひき	ます	ひいて	ひく
引きます	ひき	ます	ひいて	ひく
降ります [あめが～]	ふり	ます	ふって	ふる
払います	はらい	ます	はらって	はらう
話します	はなし	ます	はなして	はなす
曲がります [みぎへ～]	まがり	ます	まがって	まがる
待ちます	まち	ます	まって	まつ
回します	まわし	ます	まわして	まわす
持ちます	もち	ます	もって	もつ
持って行きます	もっていき	ます	もっていって	もっていく
もらいます	もらい	ます	もらって	もらう
役に立ちます	やくにたち	ます	やくにたって	やくにたつ
休みます	やすみ	ます	やすんで	やすむ
休みます [かいしゃを～]	やすみ	ます	やすんで	やすむ
呼びます	よび	ます	よんで	よぶ
読みます	よみ	ます	よんで	よむ
わかります	わかり	ます	わかって	わかる
渡ります [はしを～]	わたり	ます	わたって	わたる

ない-form		た-form	meaning	lesson
のら	ない	のった	ride, get on [a train]	16
はいら	ない	はいった	enter [a coffee shop]	13
はいら	ない	はいった	enter [university]	16
はいら	ない	はいった	take [a bath]	17
はか	ない	はいた	put on [shoes, trousers, etc.]	22
はたらか	ない	はたらいた	work	4
ひか	ない	ひいた	play (stringed instrument or piano, etc.)	18
ひか	ない	ひいた	pull	23
ふら	ない	ふった	rain	14
はらわ	ない	はらった	pay	17
はなさ	ない	はなした	speak, talk	14
まがら	ない	まがった	turn [to the right]	14
また	ない	まった	wait	14
まわさ	ない	まわした	turn	23
もた	ない	もった	hold	14
もっていか	ない	もっていった	take (something)	17
もらわ	ない	もらった	receive	7
やくにたた	ない	やくにたった	be useful	21
やすま	ない	やすんだ	take a rest, take a holiday	4
やすま	ない	やすんだ	take a day off [work]	11
よば	ない	よんだ	call	14
よま	ない	よんだ	read	6
わから	ない	わかった	understand	9
わたら	ない	わたった	cross [a bridge]	23

II −group

	ます-form		て-form	dictionary form
開けます	あけ	ます	あけて	あける
あげます	あげ	ます	あげて	あげる
集めます	あつめ	ます	あつめて	あつめる
浴びます [シャワーを 〜]	あび	ます	あびて	あびる
います	い	ます	いて	いる
います [こどもが 〜]	い	ます	いて	いる
います [にほんに 〜]	い	ます	いて	いる
入れます	いれ	ます	いれて	いれる
いれます [コーヒーを 〜]	いれ	ます	いれて	いれる
生まれます	うまれ	ます	うまれて	うまれる
起きます	おき	ます	おきて	おきる
教えます	おしえ	ます	おしえて	おしえる
教えます [じゅうしょを 〜]	おしえ	ます	おしえて	おしえる
覚えます	おぼえ	ます	おぼえて	おぼえる
降ります [でんしゃを 〜]	おり	ます	おりて	おりる
換えます	かえ	ます	かえて	かえる
変えます	かえ	ます	かえて	かえる
かけます [でんわを 〜]	かけ	ます	かけて	かける
かけます [めがねを 〜]	かけ	ます	かけて	かける
借ります	かり	ます	かりて	かりる
考えます	かんがえ	ます	かんがえて	かんがえる
気をつけます [くるまに 〜]	きを つけ	ます	きを つけて	きを つける
着ます [シャツを 〜]	き	ます	きて	きる
くれます	くれ	ます	くれて	くれる
閉めます	しめ	ます	しめて	しめる
調べます	しらべ	ます	しらべて	しらべる
捨てます	すて	ます	すてて	すてる
食べます	たべ	ます	たべて	たべる
足ります	たり	ます	たりて	たりる
疲れます	つかれ	ます	つかれて	つかれる

ない-form		た-form	meaning	lesson
あけ	ない	あけた	open	14
あげ	ない	あげた	give	7
あつめ	ない	あつめた	collect, gather	18
あび	ない	あびた	take [a shower]	16
い	ない	いた	exist, be (animate things)	10
い	ない	いた	have [a child]	11
い	ない	いた	stay, be [in Japan]	11
いれ	ない	いれた	put in, insert	16
いれ	ない	いれた	make [coffee]	24
うまれ	ない	うまれた	be born	22
おき	ない	おきた	get up, wake up	4
おしえ	ない	おしえた	teach	7
おしえ	ない	おしえた	tell [an address]	14
おぼえ	ない	おぼえた	memorize	17
おり	ない	おりた	get off [a train]	16
かえ	ない	かえた	exchange, change	18
かえ	ない	かえた	change	23
かけ	ない	かけた	make [a telephone call]	7
かけ	ない	かけた	put on [glasses]	22
かり	ない	かりた	borrow	7
かんがえ	ない	かんがえた	think, consider	25
きを つけ	ない	きを つけた	pay attention [to cars], take care	23
き	ない	きた	put on [shirt, etc.]	22
くれ	ない	くれた	give (me)	24
しめ	ない	しめた	close, shut	14
しらべ	ない	しらべた	check, investigate	20
すて	ない	すてた	throw away	18
たべ	ない	たべた	eat	6
たり	ない	たりた	be enough, be sufficient	21
つかれ	ない	つかれた	get tired	13

	ます-form		て-form	dictionary form
つけます	つけ	ます	つけて	つける
出かけます	でかけ	ます	でかけて	でかける
できます	でき	ます	できて	できる
出ます ［きっさてんを ～］	で	ます	でて	でる
出ます ［だいがくを ～］	で	ます	でて	でる
出ます ［おつりが ～］	で	ます	でて	でる
止めます	とめ	ます	とめて	とめる
寝ます	ね	ます	ねて	ねる
乗り換えます	のりかえ	ます	のりかえて	のりかえる
始めます	はじめ	ます	はじめて	はじめる
負けます	まけ	ます	まけて	まける
見せます	みせ	ます	みせて	みせる
見ます	み	ます	みて	みる
迎えます	むかえ	ます	むかえて	むかえる
やめます ［かいしゃを ～］	やめ	ます	やめて	やめる
忘れます	わすれ	ます	わすれて	わすれる

ない-form		た-form	meaning	lesson
つけ	ない	つけた	turn on	14
でかけ	ない	でかけた	go out	17
でき	ない	できた	be able to, can	18
で	ない	でた	go out [of a coffee shop]	13
で	ない	でた	graduate from [university]	16
で	ない	でた	[change] come out	23
とめ	ない	とめた	stop, park	14
ね	ない	ねた	sleep, go to bed	4
のりかえ	ない	のりかえた	change (trains, etc.)	16
はじめ	ない	はじめた	start, begin	14
まけ	ない	まけた	lose, be beaten	21
みせ	ない	みせた	show	14
み	ない	みた	see, look at, watch	6
むかえ	ない	むかえた	go to meet, welcome	13
やめ	ない	やめた	quit or retire from [a company], give up	16
わすれ	ない	わすれた	forget	17

III－group

	ます-form		て-form	dictionary form
案内します	あんないし	ます	あんないして	あんないする
運転します	うんてんし	ます	うんてんして	うんてんする
買い物します	かいものし	ます	かいものして	かいものする
来ます	き	ます	きて	くる
結婚します	けっこんし	ます	けっこんして	けっこんする
見学します	けんがくし	ます	けんがくして	けんがくする
研究します	けんきゅうし	ます	けんきゅうして	けんきゅうする
コピーします	コピーし	ます	コピーして	コピーする
散歩します [こうえんを～]	さんぽし	ます	さんぽして	さんぽする
残業します	ざんぎょうし	ます	ざんぎょうして	ざんぎょうする
します	し	ます	して	する
修理します	しゅうりし	ます	しゅうりして	しゅうりする
出張します	しゅっちょうし	ます	しゅっちょうして	しゅっちょうする
紹介します	しょうかいし	ます	しょうかいして	しょうかいする
食事します	しょくじし	ます	しょくじして	しょくじする
心配します	しんぱいし	ます	しんぱいして	しんぱいする
説明します	せつめいし	ます	せつめいして	せつめいする
洗濯します	せんたくし	ます	せんたくして	せんたくする
掃除します	そうじし	ます	そうじして	そうじする
連れて来ます	つれてき	ます	つれてきて	つれてくる
電話します	でんわし	ます	でんわして	でんわする
引っ越しします	ひっこしし	ます	ひっこしして	ひっこしする
勉強します	べんきょうし	ます	べんきょうして	べんきょうする
持って来ます	もってき	ます	もってきて	もってくる
予約します	よやくし	ます	よやくして	よやくする
留学します	りゅうがくし	ます	りゅうがくして	りゅうがくする
練習します	れんしゅうし	ます	れんしゅうして	れんしゅうする

ない-form		た-form	meaning	lesson
あんないし	ない	あんないした	show around, show the way	24
うんてんし	ない	うんてんした	drive	18
かいものし	ない	かいものした	do shopping	13
こ	ない	きた	come	5
けっこんし	ない	けっこんした	marry, get married	13
けんがくし	ない	けんがくした	visit some place for study	18
けんきゅうし	ない	けんきゅうした	do research	15
コピーし	ない	コピーした	copy	14
さんぽし	ない	さんぽした	take a walk [in a park]	13
ざんぎょうし	ない	ざんぎょうした	work overtime	17
し	ない	した	do	6
しゅうりし	ない	しゅうりした	repair	20
しゅっちょうし	ない	しゅっちょうした	go on a business trip	17
しょうかいし	ない	しょうかいした	introduce	24
しょくじし	ない	しょくじした	have a meal, dine	13
しんぱいし	ない	しんぱいした	worry	17
せつめいし	ない	せつめいした	explain	24
せんたくし	ない	せんたくした	wash (clothes)	19
そうじし	ない	そうじした	clean (a room)	19
つれてこ	ない	つれてきた	bring (someone)	24
でんわし	ない	でんわした	phone	20
ひっこしし	ない	ひっこしした	move (house)	23
べんきょうし	ない	べんきょうした	study	4
もってこ	ない	もってきた	bring (something)	17
よやくし	ない	よやくした	reserve, book	18
りゅうがくし	ない	りゅうがくした	study abroad	25
れんしゅうし	ない	れんしゅうした	practice	19

189

Contributors

田中よね　*Yone Tanaka*
The Association for Overseas Technical Scholarship
Matsushita Electric Industrial Co., LTD. Overseas Training Center
Coordinator of Japanese Language Course

牧野昭子　*Akiko Makino*
The Association for Overseas Technical Scholarship
The Japan Foundation Japanese-Language Institute, Kansai

重川明美　*Akemi Shigekawa*
The Association for Overseas Technical Scholarship
Matsushita Electric Industrial Co., LTD. Overseas Training Center

御子神慶子　*Keiko Mikogami*
The Association for Overseas Technical Scholarship
Matsushita Electric Industrial Co., LTD. Overseas Training Center

古賀千世子　*Chiseko Koga*
Kobe University International Students Center
Matsushita Electric Industrial Co., LTD. Overseas Training Center

石井千尋　*Chihiro Ishii*
YWCA Teachers' Association

Editorial Advisors

石沢弘子　*Hiroko Ishizawa*
The Association for Overseas Technical Scholarship

豊田宗周　*Munechika Toyoda*
The Association for Overseas Technical Scholarship

Illustrator

田辺瀞羊　*Kiyomi Tanabe*

写真提供
©オリオンプレス
栃木県
姫路市
広島県

**みんなの日本語　初級I
翻訳・文法解説　英語版**

1998年3月16日　初版第1刷発行
2005年2月25日　第 9 刷 発 行

編著者　　株式会社 スリーエーネットワーク
発行者　　髙井道博
発　行　　株式会社 スリーエーネットワーク
　　　　　〒101-0064 東京都千代田区猿楽町2-6-3 （松栄ビル）
　　　　　電話　営業 03(3292)5751
　　　　　　　　編集 03(3292)6521
　　　　　http://www.3anet.co.jp

印　刷　　日本印刷株式会社

不許複製　　　　　　　　ISBN4-88319-107-9 C0081
落丁・乱丁本はお取替えいたします。

初級日本語教材の定番 みんなの日本語シリーズ

みんなの日本語初級 I

本冊	2,625円	漢字英語版	1,890円
本冊・ローマ字版	2,625円	漢字カードブック	630円
翻訳・文法解説ローマ字版（英語）	2,100円	初級で読めるトピック25	1,470円
翻訳・文法解説英語版	2,100円	書いて覚える文型練習帳	1,365円
翻訳・文法解説中国語版	2,100円	漢字練習帳	945円
翻訳・文法解説韓国語版	2,100円	聴解タスク25	2,100円
翻訳・文法解説スペイン語版	2,100円	教え方の手引き	2,940円
翻訳・文法解説フランス語版	2,100円	練習C・会話イラストシート	2,100円
翻訳・文法解説ポルトガル語版	2,100円	導入・練習イラスト集	2,310円
翻訳・文法解説タイ語版	2,100円	カセットテープ	6,300円
翻訳・文法解説インドネシア語版	2,100円	CD	5,250円
翻訳・文法解説ロシア語版	2,100円	携帯用絵教材	6,300円
翻訳・文法解説ドイツ語版	2,100円	B4サイズ絵教材	37,800円
標準問題集	945円	会話ビデオ	10,500円

みんなの日本語初級 II

本冊	2,625円	漢字英語版	1,890円
翻訳・文法解説英語版	2,100円	初級で読めるトピック25	1,470円
翻訳・文法解説中国語版	2,100円	書いて覚える文型練習帳	1,365円
翻訳・文法解説韓国語版	2,100円	漢字練習帳	1,260円
翻訳・文法解説スペイン語版	2,100円	教え方の手引き	2,940円
翻訳・文法解説フランス語版	2,100円	練習C・会話イラストシート	2,100円
翻訳・文法解説ポルトガル語版	2,100円	導入・練習イラスト集	2,520円
翻訳・文法解説タイ語版	2,100円	カセットテープ	6,300円
翻訳・文法解説インドネシア語版	2,100円	CD	5,250円
翻訳・文法解説ロシア語版	2,100円	携帯用絵教材	6,825円
翻訳・文法解説ドイツ語版	2,100円	B4サイズ絵教材	39,900円
標準問題集	945円	会話ビデオ	10,500円

みんなの日本語初級　やさしい作文　1,260円

ホームページで
新刊や日本語セミナーを
ご案内しております
http://www.3anet.co.jp

価格は税込です　スリーエーネットワーク